IMMIGRANT SON
OF IMMIGRANTS

Dr Mohamed Hassan Salasa

Grosvenor House
Publishing Limited

This book is published by
Grosvenor House Publishing Ltd
Link House
140 The Broadway, Tolworth, Surrey, KT6 7HT.
www.grosvenorhousepublishing.co.uk

A CIP record for this book
is available from the British Library

ISBN 978-1-80381-271-7

Introduction

People are curious about their origins for all sorts of reasons, from curiosity about some member of the family, or perhaps the scandals associated with others, to confirming family legend about an exotic ancestry, and anything in between. For me it was not only this natural curiosity, having been born and bought up in apartheid South Africa, but also the need to understand the historical context of where the family came from and why branches of the family are geographically situated so disparately. What were the social, economic or political situations that caused them to move from one particular location to another?

It also struck me at some point that my father and most of his brothers, his mother and his paternal aunts and uncles died at the comparatively early age of around 60, at a time when life expectancy was increasing to the seventies and even eighties. It was obviously either "nature or nurture". As a doctor, I therefore had some curiosity about the possibility of inherited or genetic illnesses lurking within the family causing these "premature" demises. The "Cape Malay" diet, delicious as it is, is notoriously rich in saturated fats, red meat, sugar and salt, all known to be causative in myocardial disease, hypertension, stroke and diabetes. Added to this, certainly among the paternal uncles and aunts I knew, all smoked heavily, a deathly combination! So, were their early deaths attributable to their rich diet or was there some other genetic predisposition to these illnesses?

Many in the family who came to hear that I was in the process of researching the family tree expressed interest, and others have very kindly shared their knowledge of the family with me. I am very grateful to them all for their contributions and for allowing me access to their recollections and memories and the many family photos they cherish.

My interest was further stimulated by a number of personal events. After I retired from practising as a psychiatrist in December of 1997, I had the time to start the research and the gathering of the material. At that stage I had no idea that it would require so much more time and effort than I had ever imagined. I had started to do a degree in Arabic and Persian at the School of Oriental and African Studies at the University of London (SOAS for short), and as a break from my studies in the library, I would wander through the different areas of the library. It is, of course, one of the best libraries in the world for the study of the languages and cultures of Africa, the Middle East and Asia. I was particularly interested in the Africa section, which contained a wealth of material about South Africa. The material spanned the history of the country from before the advent of the European settlers to the present day. It contained many original and translated works covering subjects such as slavery, the rise of Islam in southern Africa and the immigration of the diverse peoples from the Indian sub-continent, and from as far afield as China. It was because of the diversity of the material, and the fact that it was right on my "doorstep", that I saw the possibility of a project that might occupy me when I finished my degree.

I was prompted most of all by enquiries from my two younger sisters, Rushdeyah[1] and Fowziyah,[2] about my grandparents, whom Fow had not known, because they had all died before she was born, and who Rush only vaguely remembered, because she had been very young when they died. They had "a right to know" what I knew about these people, and I began to feel that I had a duty to share what I knew with them.

Things came to a dramatic head for me at the end of 2001, when my mother had a quite severe stroke. It was the first of three strokes that eventually ended her life at the end of August 2002. When I saw her after her first stroke, and as someone medically

---

[1] People found "Rushdeyah" hard to pronounce, so they shortened her name to Rush and it has stuck.
[2] Similarly, although Fowziyah was easier to pronounce, people still shortened her name to Fow.

trained, I realised that her recovery would not be complete, if she were to recover at all, and I was in a dilemma, being in the middle of my studies at SOAS. I discussed my dilemma with the undergraduate tutor, Professor Hewitt, who was very understanding and sympathetic and suggested that I take the rest of the academic year off to deal with the situation. During the next nine months, I travelled to South Africa about four times to support my sisters and to make arrangements for my mother's care, when it became clear that she would need more care than the girls could reasonably be expected to provide on their own. Fow was living in Pretoria at the time, and she and Adnaan were flying down to Cape Town, at some expense, almost every second weekend and during the school holidays to help out as best they could. However, with both of them working and their children at school, they were quite restricted in what they could do.

Mum was still able to speak coherently after the first stroke, and at times when we were alone together we would reminisce about the past, and I think she welcomed the opportunity to talk to me about her youth and her family. I think it comforted her to be able to recall and thereby relive her early life, perhaps in some unconscious way realising that she may not recover. Sadly, I think we both realised that it was also a last opportunity for us to fill in the gaps in my knowledge of her family.

Mum and I had developed a quite different relationship after Boeja Joe,[3] also known as "Bie", died in August 1973. She had always confided things to me, but after the shock of Bie's death, we were able to talk about things in a more "adult way" than as mother and son. After Boeja Joe's death, as the only son and the eldest in the family, I had the responsibility of supporting Mum and helping raise my two minor sisters while living almost

---

[3] At the Cape people used Arabic words in an idiosyncratic way. *Boeja* is derived from the Arabic *Ab* or *Abu* meaning father. As tradition demanded, we called both our father, Joseph, and our grandfather, Saban, "Boeja". My father was nicknamed Joe, so as a confused child I apparently tried to distinguish between my father and grandfather by calling my father "Boeja Joe" and my grandfather "Boeja".

6,000 miles away in London. This shared responsibility, based on mutual trust and respect, changed our relationship into a kind of friendship, which continued to the end of her life. It must have become clear to Mum at some stage that she might not recover from the strokes, although she never said so to any of us, but I think her opening up about her early life whenever I asked was somehow related to this realisation. There was no longer any point in being secretive about the past.

As executor of Mum's will, my sisters agreed I should take charge of all of Mum's personal papers, and I should retain as many for myself as I wanted. Although Mum had destroyed a lot of her papers and personal letters, as well as photos, there were still quite a few that were of interest and that threw light on times that even *I* only vaguely remembered. I promised my sisters I would only be a "custodian" of the papers and would keep them safe and not destroy any of them, and upon my death they would revert to the remaining family. In the meantime, I had photocopies of all the important estate papers made and also copies of any photos they wanted for their own personal use. Mum had also retained copies of her parents' estate papers, as well as some of her brothers' and sister's papers. For me, meagre as they were, they were a treasure trove of information. Some of them confirmed things I already knew, while others shed light on things I had no idea of.

In the grief following Mum's death, after I had returned home to England, life seemed very bleak to me for a long while. I threw myself into my studies as best as I could, but deep down I came to realise many things. Apart from my "cousins", Ronnie Britten and his family, I was alone in this country that had become my home and where I had now lived for more years of my life than in the country of my birth. Although I had naturally formed deep and lasting relationships here and had a good circle of friends and acquaintances who loved and cared about me, and despite the long years I had lived and worked here, I was still, in the eyes of many others of my countrymen, just another immigrant. This did not much bother me as the years passed, but it did make me realise that even in South Africa, if I looked far enough back in time, we were all immigrants. The settlers from Europe in the 17th century were also immigrants. They imported slaves from their colonies in the East Indies, who were also technically immigrants. Other slaves came from East and West Africa and Madagascar. Added to this mix came the indentured labourers from southern India in the 19th century, followed by Indian traders from the west coast of India, all immigrants, so in effect I was "the immigrant son of immigrants" long before I migrated to this country. In fact, for all the appearance of solidity and tenure, the Salasas too are immigrants to South Africa!

After I gained British citizenship in 1975, I applied for a visa to visit South Africa in 1978. I had been unable to visit when Bie died in 1973 as I was still legally "stateless" and therefore without any passport. It had been a cause of great distress to me at the time, but there was nothing I could do about it. At the time, I could only travel on a refugee travel document issued by the United Nations High Commission for Refugees on condition that the country I travelled to was prepared to allow me entry on such a document, and then, as now, most countries would not allow entry for fear of the refugee refusing to leave and becoming a burden on the state. The racist South African government at the time would certainly not have allowed me entry on such a travel document. However, with a British passport I was finally granted a visa for a month, issued by the racist government, to visit my family. I was probably one of very few British citizens who were subjected to such a visa requirement, but after that first trip I was able to make the journey a few times to visit Bie's grave and to see the family.

Since the late 1980s, after the death of my father's last surviving brother, Uncle AbuBakr (Boeta[4] Kaatjie), my cousin, Mohamed Faiz, Uncle Allie's son, would joke that I was now the oldest Salasa living, and that he had to show me respect as such. In my absence abroad, he was the oldest bearing the Salasa name, and others in the family would have to show *him* the respect due

---

[4] *Boet* is an Afrikaans word for a brother.

to *me*! This made me think that I had in fact become "a repository" of family history. Of course, I had older cousins, sons and daughters of my father's sisters, who probably knew more about the family than I did, but I was the eldest son of the eldest son bearing the family name.

On my maternal side, Mum had had four brothers and a sister, all of whom had died without issue. I am, therefore, the only grandson of Mum's parents. Although I am no dynast, I did feel that for all these reasons I had an obligation to at least record what I knew or could find out. But what form would this record take? I could record a family tree in the traditional way, but as a historian on one hand, and as someone also trained in the scientific tradition on the other hand, I felt I wanted the record to be based not merely on oral history and the odd tall story but to be backed up by documentary proof as far as was possible. For me, Mum's estate papers became the starting point for my project. But it was to be more than three years before I could start the real work on it.

The project has become an ongoing one, and I hope that anyone in the family who has information and is interested will continue to contribute to it, and I hope that like all family stories the tree will grow as the family grows.

Salasa or Salassa?

SARINA SALASSA

My father, who my sister Saadia and I called "Boeja Joe", was originally named Joseph Salasa. He was named after his maternal grandfather, Joseph Stephanus, as was the custom of the day. Joseph Stephanus had married Sarina Meyer,[5] born Salassa, when her first husband, Joseph Meyer, also known as Joseph Mayrin,[6] had died. Sarina's estate papers clearly state that she was born on 1 January 1835 in Malmesbury, the daughter of Jacob Salassa and his wife Jeanetta. To date I have only been able to find records of her brother Abas Salassa. She may well have had other brothers and sisters, but none are as yet traceable in the historical records. Her birth date is significant in that this was the time of the end of slavery at the Cape. Slaves were officially "liberated" by law throughout the British Empire on 1 December 1834, a month before Sarina was born. However, they were "apprenticed" to their old owners for another four years before they were legally "free".

"Apprenticeship" was supposedly to prepare slaves for life as free men and women, but in reality it was a way of ensuring that the old slave owners still had a supply of labour for the four years after "liberation", while they made arrangements to deal with the consequences of the "liberation". In order to deal with the "problem" of thousands of liberated slaves roaming the countryside with nowhere to live and only their labour to sell, laws such as the Vagrancy Laws were introduced to restrict the movement of slaves, as a result of which many chose to remain with their former owners, working for them for a pittance in order not to fall foul of the Vagrancy Laws. This set the pattern for

---

5 MOOC 6/9/361 579 1897. Stephanus, Sarina (née Salassa). Estate Papers.
6 MOOC 6/9/370 2918 1897. Mayrin, Joseph. Death Notice.

Frederick Meyer, Hove, Sussex.

labour relations for the next 200 years.

I knew Sarina's grandson, Frederick Meyer, very well. I had met "Cousin Fred", as he was known to us all, as a child when he visited Gadija, his aunt, my paternal grandmother, at 28 Goldsmith Road, and when she died, he continued to visit his cousins on a fairly regular basis. He became valet to Sir Abe Bailey and accompanied him to the UK when he retired. After Sir Abe Bailey's death, Cousin Fred remained in England and worked in grand houses in Belgravia as a butler. His last job before he retired to Hove, Sussex, in the late 1970s was for the chairman of Lloyds Bank, who had a very large townhouse in fashionable Eaton Square, London, where I visited Cousin Fred often after going into exile in London in 1968. He and another butler shared the large and luxurious basement flat, from where they ruled the servants working in the house. He used to go to South Africa for his annual holiday, paid for by his employers, to visit his remaining family.

I don't know if Cousin Fred actually knew his grandmother, as she died in 1897, but he recalls that she was called Sophie. Just before his death around 1978/9, Ronnie's wife, Crystal, sat him down and asked him to explain the family connections between the Salasas and the Meyers. She recorded what he told her and I have used her record as a basis to trace the Meyer branch of the family. Although this was oral family history, I was soon able to trace the people mentioned by him from documents and papers in the Cape Town Archives, and the facts tallied with the legends to a remarkable extent. I am, therefore, extremely grateful to Cousin Fred for his recollections, and to Crystal who recorded what he recounted.

The Meyer side of the family know Sarina Salassa as Sophie Meyer. I think that she may well have answered to both names. Even today many people have two names. I am myself known as "Sonny" to family and friends, although my given name is Mohamed Hassan. However, in Sarina's case there may be different reasons for the ambiguity.

Slaves imported to South Africa from the Dutch East Indies in the 17th and 18th centuries from places as varied as Batavia, the Coromandel Coast of India and Ceylon, as well as Madagascar and East and West Africa, were deprived of their given names and renamed by their new masters, with names that could easily be pronounced by them. Many of these slaves held on to their given names in an effort to retain a little of their dignity, culture and religious background. It may also be that they were known by their original names to other slaves who came from the same region or were of a similar cultural or religious background. So, in effect, they would all have had two or more names—their original names and the new names given to them by the slave owner, who probably was not even aware of their original names. Even more frustratingly, their names would sometimes be changed by their new owners when they were sold on. Only the new names given to them by their owners appeared in the official records, so one is heavily dependent on oral family history in tracing individuals.

We know from the historical records that Islam had come to the Cape in the 17th century with the slaves from the Dutch colonies, and that a considerable number of slaves were Muslim, the greater part of them from the Malay Peninsula. By the 18th century the Muslim population of the Cape was exceeding the white settler population and was growing fast because of conversion. The Dutch administration had not encouraged conversion to Christianity, as this would have forced them to baptise and free the converted slaves. The settler population's literal interpretation of the Bible led them to believe that Christians could not be enslaved, so until the arrival in force of Christian missionaries in the 19th century, conversion to Islam was greater than to Christianity. In fact, it was at this time that the expression "turning Malay" originated for conversion to Islam. Even white converts to Islam were described as turning Malay! The expression survived well into the 20th century, and I remember it being used as a child. Conversion also meant taking an Arabic name or the Cape version of an Arabic name.

It is, therefore, not a surprise that Sarina may have been known by two names, but also that her parents, if they were slaves or freed slaves, also had so-called "Christian" names (Jacob and Jeanetta). I have not been able, either through the historical records or oral family history, to discover their Arabic or Muslim names.

It is, however, certain that Jacob and Jeanetta's daughter, Sarina Salassa, was born in Malmesbury, and she probably grew up there. There is no living family member who knew her personally, or anything of her early life. From the historical records, we know that she married Joseph Meyer, a small farmer in the Durbanville area, around 1850. They had a large family of nine children. The eldest boy, Jacob Paul Meyer, was born in 1851 and named after Sarina's father, Jacob Salassa. The eldest girl, Jeanetta, was named after Sarina's mother, Jeanetta. As mentioned before, this was the custom at the time in both the Dutch settler population as well as among the slave population, and is, therefore, a useful tool in working out relationships within families, when they stuck to the tradition. It becomes much more difficult to work out the relationships from the time this custom died out.

SARINA MEYER (born SALASSA) AND HER CHILDREN

We know nothing of Sarina's first husband, Joseph Meyer, how they met, and when or where they were married. He may have been quite a few years older than her. He died on 28 January 1884 in Durbanville, presumably on their farm, leaving her with nine children ranging in age from teenagers to others in their early twenties. His death notice does not give his age at his death, but she herself was only in her late forties. She married again after her first husband's death, to a Joseph Stephanus. It is again unclear who he was and how they met, but they had two further children, despite her age. The two girls were named Magdalina and Dulfina, also spelt Doelfina or Dolphina. Sarina had followed the tradition of naming her eldest two children, by Joseph Meyer, after her parents, so the question is, did she name Magdalina and Dolphina after her new husband's parents? They were aged about nine or ten when she died on 5 January 1897 at the age of about 62. It appears that the family continued to live in Sarina's house in Durbanville, but it is unclear who looked after the two younger children. Sarina's estate papers merely record that Joseph Stephanus and their children continued to live "at her property in Durbanville". The property itself consisted of a house, and some land with wells on it. It is not clear when Joseph Stephanus died or what happened to his two young daughters by Sarina after his death, or what happened to the house in Durbanville where they had all lived.

Jeanetta Maria Watham, born Meyer

Sarina's eldest daughter, Jeanetta Maria, was born around 1860 in Durbanville, presumably on her parents' farm. Little is known of her early life and childhood. She would have been around 37 when her mother died in 1897. According to Sarina's death notice, Jeanetta was present at her mother's deathbed, and it was she who gave the information contained in the death notice. As the eldest daughter she may have had some role in raising her two stepsisters, Magdalina and Dolphina, who were still minors at the time.

She married a John Peter Watham, who was born about 1860 at Klipfontein. We do not know how or when they met, but they were married in Durbanville, where she was born and probably still lived with her parents at the time. It is unclear when they moved from there, but at some stage they moved to Bellville and lived in a house off the Main Road, where according to their estate papers, they both eventually died. He had been a ganger on the railways. At the time, this job, a kind of overseer of unskilled labourers, was of the kind reserved for "poor Whites" who had no formal education or qualifications. His parents, according to his death notice, were William Henry Watham and Johanna Watham.[7] I have yet to find

---

[7] MOOC 6/9/1877 10 1921, John Peter Watham. Estate Papers.

out more about them in the historical records. He died on 27 December 1920. She never remarried and died on 12 August 1930 at their home in Bellville. For the record, her death notice confirms that her parents were Joseph and Selina (Sarina).[8]

Jeanetta and Peter had five children—Selina Elizabeth, Johanna Maria, Elizabeth Sophia, William Henry and Joseph Henry—and an adopted son, called Peter Simon. Selina Elizabeth was obviously named after her maternal grandmother. There is not much of a difference between "Sarina" and "Selina", and then, as now, people often misspelled names. Johanna Maria was named after her paternal grandmother, Johanna Watham. It is possible that Eliza Sophia was named after her maternal grandmother, Sarina Salassa, by the latter's other name, Sophie. So it seems that the couple conformed to the convention of naming their children after their own parents and grandparents!

Their eldest son, Henry William, was named exactly after his paternal grandfather, William Henry Watham, while the second son, Joseph Henry, was named after his maternal grandfather, Joseph Meyer. The naming of the children in this case, therefore, ran true to custom. With a large family of their own, it is interesting that they adopted another child, Peter Simon. Was it just altruism or was he the offspring of another family member who for some reason was unable to raise the child themselves?

Jacob Paul Meyer

Sarina's eldest son, Jacob Paul, was said to have been born in 1851, which would have meant that she was just 16 when he was born. If the dates are correct, she was married very young and her husband, Joseph Meyer, would have been much older than she was. Such disparages in age on marriage were not unknown at the time. Another possibility was that Joseph Meyer had been married before, and that Sarina was his second wife.

---

[8] Death Notice. Jeanetta Maria Watham, born Meyer.

Not much is known about Jacob Paul except that he too was a small farmer in the Durbanville area. We do not know if he inherited his father's farm or whether he bought this farm himself. He married Margaret Scholtz and they had six children—James, Sally, Sophie, John, Frederick (known to me as Cousin Fred) and John Essack. According to Cousin Fred, the farm did not do well, so the couple sold it and left, first for the diamond mines at Kimberly and then to the goldmines on the Rand, to try to better themselves. While in Johannesburg and while her husband was at the Cape stranded during the Anglo–Boer War (1899–1902), Margaret gave birth to her youngest child, John Essack. She "gave" the child to a court interpreter called Cassiem in either Johannesburg or Pretoria; Cousin Fred was not sure which of the two cities it was.

Rather confusingly, there were two brothers named John—a John and a John Essack—in the family. I suspect that John Essack remained in Johannesburg and grew up there but maintained contact with his brothers and sisters in the Cape. As a child, I had also heard that Sally, one of the sisters, had married, lived and died in Johannesburg. She had a son called James, who appears to have been quite a strong character, and I remember a rumour, when Cousin Fred died, that he was determined to come to England to claim his inheritance from his uncle! Nothing came of it, as Cousin Fred had distributed whatever he had accumulated during his lifetime, so there was no "inheritance" to claim!

Whenever Cousin Fred visited South Africa, he would make a point of seeing James in Johannesburg, but he usually stayed with his niece, Loma, James's sister, who lived in Cape Town. She was a floor manager for Stuttafords, then a very classy and expensive department store in the main shopping area in Adderley Street, Cape Town, and later, when the store moved to one of the early shopping malls, in Cavendish Square, Claremont. It was a very prestigious job usually reserved for Whites, and although Loma was dark complexioned, she was obviously very good at her job and well thought of. Mum, who liked Loma very much, would look her up whenever she shopped in Stuttafords.

John Meyer

John Meyer was adopted by his paternal aunt, Eliza Meyer, also known as "Hatta" to Cousin Fred. She was married to Abraham Ontong, so John became known as John/Johnnie Ontong. His two stepsisters were known as Auntie Pop and Auntie Sentie. They lived at Durbanville and as far as I know never married. I remember as a child visiting them in Durbanville with my parents. They were two charming sisters, a little bit eccentric but very kind and hospitable. They died in the 1970s. Their father, Abraham Ontong, died on 19 February 1937. His wife, Eliza, died three years later on 23 December 1940, and they are buried side by side in Durbanville in the White cemetery. Rush and I came across their grave quite by chance while wandering through the graveyard in 2007. Their graves are still well tended, with a marble headstone giving their death dates. It was apparently erected by a "friend", Mrs Louw. It is a mystery to me who she was and what the nature of their friendship was, but it must have been a deep one for her to have spent so much money on a marble headstone for their graves. The fact that the graves were so well kept made me wonder if there were still descendents of the couple living in the area tending the graves.

Sophie Sortel, born Meyer (Ronnie Britten's grandmother)

Jacob Paul's daughter, Sophie Meyer, was either named after her mother, Sophie Scholtz, or her paternal grandmother, Sarina/ Sophie Salassa. Oral history has it that she was a very fair complexioned old lady, who was also a little eccentric. She married Montague Sortel, and the couple had only one child, a daughter called Margaret Mary Ann, known to me as "Cousin Margaret". They lived in Paarl, the centre of the

Cousin Margaret and Sonny, circa 1978.

winegrowing region of the Western Cape. Cousin Margaret was short in stature and very fair in complexion, with brown eyes, and apparently very like her mother. She married Willem John Britten, a local postman, and they lived in a beautiful house in Berg Street, just below the Paarl Rock[9] and overlooking the Paarl Valley. The house had a large garden and a wonderful orchard, which my uncles and aunts raided whenever they visited. The family had to move from this idyllic home when the area was declared a "White" residential area under the notorious Group Areas Act. It is today the site of a very prestigious five-star hotel called La Grande Roche. Cousin Margaret and her husband were frequent visitors to Salt River. They would telephone ahead to let us know when they were visiting, and various of my aunts would make Malay food to entertain them.

Mum was particularly fond of them both, and particularly of Cousin Willie because of his wicked sense of humour! He would drive a car, a rare event in those days when few people owned cars. When he came to the corner of Tennyson Steet and Goldsmith Road, he would let one of his sons out of the car to look out for oncoming traffic. It was always a source of great amusement for us to watch this performance! Cousin Willie died tragically of cancer in the 1970s.[10] Cousin Margaret never remarried. As she grew older she became

Margaret Britten with Sonny and Mum in the former's back garden in Paarl, December 1978.

[9] Voters' Roll 1931 (Paarl) 645 Britten, William John. Berg Street. Postman. Joint tenant. Voters' Roll 1931 (Paarl) 644 Britten, Charles. Berg Street. Fruit Dealer. Sole tenant.
[10] Willem John Britten. Will Number 5020/75.

increasingly deaf but insisted on living on her own despite her increasing frailty. She eventually compromised by agreeing to live on her own in a house in Paarl, next to her eldest daughter, Olive. It was here that I visited her on one of my visits to South Africa. She had insisted on laying out a table for tea and had baked a cake for the occasion. She would not allow Olive to help in any of the preparations or in serving the tea! She died of a heart attack on 18 August 1987.[11]

Cousin Margaret and Cousin Willie had six children—Montague/Monty (named after his maternal grandfather), Ronald John/Ronnie, Gilbert, Olive, Lorraine and Frederick/Freddy (named after his maternal great-uncle, who I knew as Cousin Fred). Monty was born on 11 July 1926 and was a teacher. He died in June 2007, and his wife, Grace, and their children still live in Wellington.

Ronnie was born on 26 May 1929 and grew up and taught for some years in Paarl. He had been to the University of Cape Town and was probably the first of our family to go to university, at a time when few could afford to do so. He was greatly involved in politics and, therefore, a target for the racist government's secret police. He just avoided arrest by escaping across the border to Botswana on foot, and after a very long and painful odyssey through various African countries as a refugee was given political asylum in Britain. I don't remember meeting Ronnie in South Africa, but when I arrived in Britain, Cousin Fred urged me to visit him and his wife, Crystal. They invited me to their home in Hemel Hempstead and we became close friends and have remained so after all these years. Shortly after our first meeting, I got my first "permanent" job in Britain, at a large Victorian psychiatric hospital in St Albans called Hill End Hospital, about six miles east of Hemel Hempstead, so we were able to visit each other frequently, which further cemented our friendship.

---

[11] Death Certificate Number 6357. Margaret Mary Anne Britten. Died 18 August 1987.

Ronnie, Crystal and Ronald. Hill End Hospital St Albans, 1969.

Ronnie is about 5ft 10in and fair like his mother. He has always had a lively intellect and does not suffer fools gladly. He is extremely well read and has retained his keen interest in politics. His wife, Crystal, trained as a nurse with Ronnie's sister, Lorraine, and it was this friendship that led to their first meeting and their eventual marriage.

Ronald Britten, Hemel Hempstead.

They have only one child, a son, Ronald Ashton. Ronald was born and grew up in Hemel Hempstead. His first marriage unfortunately ended in divorce, but he has a son, Derrick, born in May 1996, from the marriage. Ronald married Holly in early 2008 and they have a daughter Darcey, born on 25 November 2008, and a second daughter, Nell, born in the Spring of 2010.

I do not remember ever meeting Gilbert or Freddie, Cousin Margaret's two other sons. Freddie died on 11 July 2006. His wife, Janice, and their children still live in South Africa. Gilbert died rather tragically in a drowning accident when I was still a child. I believe that his wife, Marie, still lives in South Africa.

Of all Cousin Margaret's children, the eldest, Olive, was the most shy and reserved. She was married to Ashton Morris. I first met her on a visit to South Africa in the 1980s, after her father had died and Cousin Margaret had moved into the house next to hers in Paarl. The arrangement was made so that Olive could "look in" on Cousin Margaret, who at this stage insisted on living on her own, despite her increasing frailty and deafness. I have a photo of the occasion of us in Cousin Margaret's garden. The next occasion I met Olive and her husband was on a visit to Centurion in Pretoria, where Fow and Adnaan had moved to because of Adnaan's work. Fow had had to have an operation on a slipped cervical vertebral disc, and after the operation Olive and Ashton, who were on a visit to Pretoria to see their daughter and her husband, came to tea at Fow's. Sadly, Ashton developed Alzheimer's disease and died in March 2007. Olive herself developed cancer of the colon and has had a successful colectomy. She seems to be doing well.

Cousin Margaret's youngest daughter is Lorraine. She is short in stature, fair and has a wicked sense of humour. Lorraine and Crystal trained as nurses in Somerset Hospital, where some years later I also spent time as a medical student. She married Frank Anthony, another

Lorraine Anthony/Britten and Rush.

political activist of the Apartheid era. Unfortunately, he was arrested and imprisoned on Robben Island for several years. Lorraine was left to raise their two daughters, Lynne and Renèe, on her own. She worked at the Tygerberg Hospital and rose to become matron until she retired. I had not known her in South Africa but met her on her

Lorraine's sister-in-law Mel, Lorraine and Crystal Britten, Alexandra Park Road, 2006.

visits to Britain to see Ronnie and Crystal, and we have become great friends; so much so that whenever I am in South Africa I make a point of visiting her at her home in Brackenfell. Frank was eventually released from prison, but the couple like many others, had been driven apart by the years of their enforced separation. They divorced, and rather tragically Frank developed cancer shortly after and died.

Clara Susanna de Mink, born Meyer

Sarina's last daughter by Joseph Meyer was Clara Susanna Meyer. She was born around 1864 and grew up with her brothers and sisters on their parents' farm in Durbanville. In her case too I have been unable to discover much about her early life. Her death notice gives her father as Joseph and her mother as "Sernia", obviously a misspelling of Sarina. She had been married to Hermanus Jacobus de Mink, and the couple lived at Wellington Road, Durbanville, until their deaths. Hermanus died on 22 October 1924 at the age of 64 years and 6 months, which means that he was born around 1860. His parents were Marinus and Janneta de Mink, but apart from this I have been unable to find out anything else about him. The couple had seven children— Selina (obviously named after her maternal grandmother, Sarina Salassa), Joseph Jacobus (named after his maternal grandfather, Joseph Meyer), Catherina, Hermanus Stephanus, Elizabeth Sophia, Adam Stephanus and Evelyn Elizabeth.

The eldest daughter, Selina, was born around 1885, so she would have been around 12 years old when her maternal grandmother, Sarina, died, and three years older than her step-aunt, Gadija Salasa, my grandmother. Little else is known about Selina except that she married Robert Dennis and was already a widow when her mother, Clara Susanna, died in 1940.

It is unclear if Clara Susanna's eldest son married, but he was appointed executor dative for his father's estate, when the latter died in 1924.[12] The estate papers mention that he lived at 7 de Smidt Street, Cape Town.

The next child, Catherina de Mink was a spinster.

The youngest son, Adam Stephanus de Mink, was made executor of his mother's estate in her will. The reason is unclear, unless his older brother had died by this stage. Nothing else is mentioned about the other children, except the youngest daughter, Evelyn Elizabeth de Mink, born in 1905, who was 19 when her father died. When her mother died in 1940, she would have been 35 years old. Her mother's death notice has it that by this time Evelyn was married to Alfred George. My mother met her shortly after her own wedding and described Evelyn as a very elegant and refined woman, whom she was very fond of. She was the only person in South Africa, other than Mum, who, as a child, I knew to possess a fur coat!

Dolphina Francina Carolina Foulding, born Stephanus

Sarina Salassa's second daughter by Joseph Stephanus was Dolphina Francina Carolina, born around 1881, which makes her about seven years older than her sister, Magdalina/Gadija Salassa. Like all of Sarina's children, she too was born at Durbanville, but moved to Hope Street, Belleville, on her marriage to Pieter Joseph George Fouldien. He died on 25 October 1942. She herself died about two years later, on 14 December 1944, at their home, "Mayfair", in Hope Street, Bellville. The couple had three

---

12 MOOC 6/9/2783 7697 1925, Hermanus Jacobus de Mink. Estate Papers.

children—George Johannes Pieter, Joseph Jacobus (perhaps named after his maternal grandfather) and John Smith.

There are still many Fouldings in the Cape Town telephone directory, and even a Muslim family who spell their name Fouldien, which may be a corruption of Foulding.

ABAS SALASSA AND HIS DESCENDENTS

Sarina's brother, Abas Salassa, is the most directly traceable of the Salassa ancestors. It is unclear whether he or his sister was the elder, but I suspect that Sarina was the elder because she died in 1897, whereas Abas was certainly still alive about 20 years later, in 1921. Again, we know very little about his early life in Malmesbury, where both he and Sarina were born. I have been unable to find his death notice in the Cape Town Archival Repository, but there is a mortgage bond dated 1899 in his name for a property in Malmesbury. The family, therefore, have very clear connections with Malmesbury, and it is probably where Abas and Sarina grew up. Oral history has it that he married Soliha (or Gassia), the daughter of a Bengali man and a French–Creole woman (see "The Brown Connection" below).

We know from the historical records that in the 18th century the Dutch introduced slaves directly from Bengal and the Coromandel Coast of India to the Cape, but the French–Creole connection is slightly unusual. We also know that Dutch ships on their way back to Holland from Batavia often stopped for victuals at the island of Mauritius. The island had been settled by the Dutch early in the 17th century but abandoned in 1710 because of the harsh climate. The French from the neighbouring island of Rèunion then took and settled the island in 1715, and the island remained French until the British took it after the Napoleonic Wars. The French had developed the sugar industry on Mauritius, for which they used slave labour, and as a result of the mixture of French culture and that of the slaves, a Creole culture emerged. It is presumably from this origin that Soliha/Gassia came. We do not know anything about her parents or how or when she came to the Cape, or indeed whether she might have been born in the Cape.

Oral family history has it that she had previously been married to Rajab Brandt (the family changed their name in the early 20th century to Brown), and when he died she married Abas Salassa from Malmesbury. The couple had six children—Rajab, Saban, Asa, Abdol and Francina Georgina. All of the children's death notices give their parents as being Abas and Gassia and their place of birth as Malmesbury. There was another child only obliquely mentioned in the record, and whose death notice I have been unable to trace. She was Sabria or Sabreyya. Of all of Abas's children, only Sabreyya, Saban and Abdol had any offspring, and all the contemporary Salasa family descend from Abas's younger son, Saban.

SABREYYA AND HER DESCENDENTS

Sabreyya may have died young, shortly after she married Abdol Mallick Majiet, by whom she had two children—Abdol Karriem and Gassia (or Gassie). I am unsure of what happened to Abdol Mallick because no one I knew ever talked about him, and he and his wife seem to have disappeared from the historical records. The children were obviously quite small when their parents disappeared from the records, for their maternal uncle, Saban Salasa, and his wife, Gadija, fostered Abdol Karriem. He chose to take their surname and became known as Karriem Salasa, a cause of great confusion in the family.

Karriem Salasa/Majiet,
circa 1953.

Karriem married Rachmat Kriel and they set up home obliquely opposite 59 Fenton Road, our first family home, and where descendents of their family still live. Karriem was about 5ft 10in in height. He was dark in complexion and had a mole on one of his cheeks. There is a photo of him taken in the 1950s with Mum's brother-in-law, Frank Cooper, who was visiting us at the time. He is dressed as he usually was, in a suit with open shirt collar and wearing a red fez. He held strong opinions about many things and did not hesitate to express them. Although he prided himself in his "Salasa heritage", he would sometimes freely admit that he was in fact a Majiet, and not a Salasa.

I do not know if he was old enough to remember his maternal grandparents, Abas and Soliha, but he put forward the view that he and his cousins (my father and his brothers and sisters) were "of Bengali descent". I do not know what he based this assumption on, but as I pointed out before, other family members certainly believed that Soliha was the daughter of a Bengali man and a French–Creole woman, so in fact they may well have had "Bengali blood".

Rachmat Kriel came from the Kriel family. She was about 5ft 8in in height and very fair in complexion. She had a very agreeable disposition and was long suffering, as I don't think that Karriem was an easy man to get on with. The couple had seven children who survived into adult life. Moegsien, the eldest, married his maternal uncle, Hadjie Mohamed Salie Kriel's, divorced second wife, Farieda, a marriage that was much disapproved of in the family, but the couple seemed happy. Hadjie Mogamat Salie's first wife, Hadjie Salma, lived in one of the two-storey houses at the bottom of Fenton Road with her only daughter and two grandsons, one of whom went to school with me at Habibia. The elder boy had cerebral palsy and was epileptic. He went to the special school at Wittebome. Hadjie Salma was a very fair and beautiful woman and Mum really liked her. She may well have been a convert to Islam, but after her conversion she observed all the customs and practices of her new faith. After Gadija Salasa died, it was mooted that she might marry my grandfather, Saban, but nothing came of it. Moegsien's wife, Farieda, died on 19 October 1989.[13]

Karriem and Rachmat had two daughters—Rugaya and Mymona. Their sons were AbuBakr (nicknamed "Akkers"), Abdurahman (nicknamed "Maanie"), Omar (nicknamed "Bokka") and the youngest, Ebrahim. Omar was about two years older than Ebrahim, and the latter was about the same age as I was, so we

---

[13] Death Certificate Number 9078.

naturally became friends. Omar kept pigeons, of which he was very fond, and the best way to upset him was to disturb them when they were broody! He became involved in the Scientology movement in the 1960s, but I don't know what became of this interest. He first married Mona Richards, a woman much older than himself. I know they had a son called Mogammad Ta-Yib, whose wife, Tasmeem, works in the Administration Department at the University of Cape Town.

Omar separated from his first wife and remarried. I have been in email contact with two of his daughters by his second marriage, Aneeqa and Gadeeja-Sabbreyah, as he was very interested in the family's history and had made many notes, which I have unfortunately not been able to consult. Omar died of cancer on 18 January 1999.[14] His daughter, Gadeeja-Sabbreyyah, was presumably named after his paternal grandmother, Sabreyya Salassa. Gadeeja-Sabreyya had not actually seen her father's notes, but she had her own theory that the family came from the Hadramout in southern Arabia, where she knew of a tribe of Salasas.

When Karriem Salasa's daughter Rugaya married, my sister Saadia was a flower girl in the wedding procession. Mum's copy of a photo of Saadia in the dress she wore for the wedding has been lost. Saadia was about five at the time of the wedding. I also remember Mymona's wedding. At the time, her maternal grandmother, *Ouma* (Grandmother) Kriel, who was staying with them, died unexpectedly on the morning of the wedding. The Sheikhs and Imams who were consulted as to whether the wedding should be postponed ruled that it should go ahead despite the fact that the funeral would also have to take place in the same house on that day. Also living with the family in Fenton Road at that time was Gassia, Karriem's sister. She was also called "Motta". I have no idea what the word means. She was, I think, unmarried, and towards the end of her life lived with one of her nephews (her brother's son) in Chatham Road. Fow recalls that she died when she, Fow, was about six or seven years old, around 1968.

---

[14] Death Certificate Number 896.

RAJAB SALASSA

Very little is known about Abas's eldest son, Rajab Salassa, although he must have been pivotal in the family's fortunes. I do not know if he was the "bachelor uncle" that Auntie Loema (see "The Brown Connection") sometimes referred to. His death notice confirms that he was born in Malmesbury, like all his brothers and sisters. It is unclear when he moved to Cape Town and whether he moved with the rest of the family or on his own. He was 60 years old when he died on 20 July, 1935, which means that he was born around 1865, confirming him as the eldest of Abas's children. His death notice[15] gives his occupation as mason and states that he was unmarried. He must have been quite successful in life, as he owned 24, 26 and 28 Goldsmith Road, although he may have inherited 28 from his father, Abas. I suspect he owned the properties in his own right, as Abas would have made a will stipulating that his (Abas's) estate be divided among all his children. I have found no such will, nor a liquidation and distribution account, after Abas's death, so one must assume that Rajab acquired the properties in his own right. He died intestate, so his properties were sold by public auction to his surviving brother, Saban Salassa, and his sister, Asa van Witt, for £490. The estate was divided between his brother (Saban) and surviving sister (Asa) and the son (Karriem Salasa) of their deceased sister, Sabbreya (or Sabria). Each received £87 and 5 shillings and 10 pence! This was a considerable amount of money in those days.

SABAN SALASA, or "BOEJA"

Saban Salassa was born on 12 November 1886 in Malmesbury, where he grew up. We know little about his childhood and early life. He probably learnt his trade as a bricklayer from his father, as was the custom of the day. He married his first cousin, Magdalina Stephanus, the daughter of his father's sister, Sarina Salassa. Magdalina was born around 1888 in Durbanville, where her

---

[15] MOOC 6/9/4657 47125 1935. Salassa, Rajab. Estate Papers.

Gadija Salasa—possibly the lady in the white veil.

parents were small farmers (see above). The date of their marriage is not certain. She converted to Islam on her marriage and became Gadija Salasa.[16] I knew both of my grandparents as a child. Gadija, or Ummie[17] as all her children and grandchildren called her, was about 5ft 8in in height. She always wore ankle-length dresses and at home wore a scarf that covered her hair. When going out she would always be veiled and even wore gloves. I have one photo of her with two relations. They are all veiled and one cannot tell them apart! She would sometimes entertain her relations from Durbanville and Malmesbury, who were always invited to family functions, like weddings, when a special table would be set aside for them. Even with them she would be veiled and would even kiss them through the veil. Occasionally, we would all go to visit the family, who, because she was so observant of her new religion, made it a point to let us know that whatever food they served us was Halal.

Ummie was very fair in complexion and had deep blue-green eyes. She had small fat deposits in the pouches beneath her eyes, which I now know to have been a sign of a high blood cholesterol level. She was quite gentle in nature, although she was able to effectively discipline her children. Like many people coming from the country she retained a love of growing things. I remember the front garden at 28 Goldsmith Road always having flowers. In the backyard she had a grapevine that trailed over a trellis that covered the first part of the backyard. I can remember seeing the grapes, tantalisingly out of reach for someone of my stature when I was five or six! I also remember that she kept a chicken or two. Also in the

---

[16] Death Certificate C79 3313 Gadija Salasa. Died 17 September 1948.

[17] *Ummie* is derived from the Arabic *Umm*, meaning mother. *Ummie*, therefore, means "my mother". Over the years this word has come to be used for any older woman.

backyard was the fig tree, allegedly planted by Saban's father, Abas, from a cutting taken at Malmesbury. The tree was unusual because it bore white-fleshed figs, while our neighbours' trees all bore purple fruit. The tree survived until the late 1990s, and although it was dying of what looked like a fungal infection, it bore fruit to the end. Rush eventually had to have someone to cut it down, although every year since then it continues to produce shoots!

Saban was a tall man, about 6ft 1in or 6ft 2in in height. He rolled his r's like the French do, a characteristic, at the time, of people coming from Malmesbury and the surrounding

**Saban Salassa,
Darling Street, Cape Town,
circa 1945.**

areas. Some people made fun of the accent. He always dressed in a shirt, waistcoat or jumper, and a jacket, and wore a red fez. The "movie snap" photo of him walking along a very recognisable Darling Street in Cape Town is exactly how I remember him. He was edentulous and never wore dentures as far as I can remember. He smoked roll-ups and smelled of tobacco. Although a bricklayer by trade, by the time I knew him he no longer worked full time. He tended to work with his sons, who were all bricklayers, except for uncle AbuBakr (Kagee), who was always rather delicate physically. All the brothers seemed to work together on most of their jobs, forming a "gang". One of the last jobs Saban worked on was the building of the shop, the dairy and the flat above the shop opposite 28 Goldsmith Road, for an Indian trader named Ma'mun Dalvi. At the time it was one of the most modern buildings in Salt River, with brick-glass partitions and terrazo floors.

Saban Salassa's identity card, 1956.

Following his brother Rajab's death, Saban and his sister Asa had bought 24, 26 and 28 Goldsmith Road together, and on Asa's death Saban owned the properties outright. Saban sold 24 and 26 Goldsmith Road to Ebrahim Kamalodien in December 1944[18] for the sum of £1,100. Both of the properties have remained in that family up to the time of writing. I have no idea what the circumstances were that made him sell the properties, whether it was the hardships of the war years, when there was little building work, or whether it was just that he felt he wanted to retire and have the money from the sale to live on. There was no State Pension scheme for non-Whites at the time.

He did make some renovations to 28 Goldsmith Road shortly after this. He laid out the front *stoep* and the path leading up to the front door and replaced the boundary fences with moulded walls. Only the walls flanking the path to the front door and enclosing the *stoep* have survived.

"La Belle", 28 Goldsmith Road, Salt River, Cape Town, 2007.

The outer walls had to be replaced after a car damaged the wall on the Tennyson Street side in 1958,[19] and Boeja Joe decided that he wanted the outer walls fronting the pavement to be symmetrical and the same. It was Saban who decided to call 28 Goldsmith Road "La Belle" ("The Beautiful" in French). I don't know if for him there was a connection with a place or a farm of that name that he wanted to commemorate. As far as I know, no one in the family spoke French, and everyone speculated on the meaning of "La Belle".

On pay day every Friday evening, my father sent me down to Goldsmith Road with an envelope containing a small paper

---

[18] Deed of Transfer No 1396 29 January 1945.
[19] KAB 3/CT 4/2/1/3/4024 B4145 1958. Damaged boundary wall 28 Goldsmith Road.

money note, with instructions to give it to Saban, who would put it unopened into his waistcoat pocket, sit me on his knee and ask me about school and what I had learnt that week. I had to recount all the stories I had learnt, and my way of relating them caused a great deal of amusement to the adults! I would be rewarded with a penny to spend on sweets!

We also visited as a family on a Sunday afternoon for afternoon tea. Ummie would try to get us to have large pieces of cake, which Mum had forewarned us to refuse, so as not to give the impression we were hungry or did not have food at home! It was difficult to resist. Ummie was present at Saadia's birth and gave a pre-arranged signal to Boeja Joe, who was playing with me in the backyard of our house at 59 Fenton Road, to announce that the baby had been born.

Ummie suffered from high blood pressure and had a heart attack and died on 17 September 1948, at the age of 60. Her death certificate gives the cause of death as coronary thrombosis, hypertension and chronic nephritis, which it says she suffered from during the previous 20 months. It also stated that a J. Salasa (Joseph Salasa, my father) would be responsible for her burial! Hers was the first funeral I ever attended. I was five going on six at the time. Saban never remarried. I have mentioned the one occasion when it was proposed that he marry the divorced sister-in-law of Karriem Salasa's wife, but it came to nothing because of reluctance on his part. Saban himself died of a heart attack on 7 October 1955,[20] when I was about 12 years old.

It is unclear exactly when the family moved from Malmesbury to Cape Town, but there is a deed of transfer for the properties 24–28 Goldsmith Road to Abas Salassa dated 31 January 1921,[21] which suggests a probable date for his move to Salt River. The document states that he paid £900 sterling for all three of the properties. The properties passed to Abas's older son, Rajab Salassa, the following year by a deed of transfer dated 24 March

[20] Death Notice 6973 Saban Salasa. Died 7 October 1955.
[21] Deed of Transfer No 3604 9 March 1921.

1922,[22] for the sum of £450 sterling. It, therefore, seems as if Abas died in either 1921 or 1922 and that Rajab either inherited the properties or bought them from his father's estate. Abas is buried in the Observatory Muslim Cemetery, where subsequently Saban and Boeja Joe were also buried in the same grave. I have no proof, but I suspect that it is also the grave where Rajab is buried.

Oral history has it that when the family moved to Cape Town, Saban and Gadija rented accommodation in District Six, in Cross Street to be exact, and this was where Boeja Joe was born on 11 November 1915. There is also a story that the family then moved to Fenton Road. The family were going through hard times as my uncles and aunts were still infants, so Saban's step-cousins, Tape Brown and his wife Gadija, fostered Boeja Joe for a while. Boeja Joe always considered Gadija Brown to be his "second mother". She died on 30 May 1973,[23] about two months before him. Everyone remarked on how devastated he had been at her death.

ABDOL SALASSA

I have not been able to discover a great deal about Abas Salassa's third son, Abdol. He was obviously the middle son, born after Rajab but before Saban. There is a mortgage bond in his name on a property in Malmesbury dated 1899,[24] but I have not been able to find out any more about him except that he did have a daughter, Ameena Salassa (or Ameena Abdol). She married an Ismail Mohammad Kasu from Malmesbury. His death notice in 1941[25] states that she died around 1920, after which he married again, a certain Gadeja Brown, the daughter of Rajab Brandt/Brown. Ismail Kasu and Ameena lived in Malmesbury[26] and had two

---

[22] Deed of Transfer No 2451 24 March 1922.
[23] Death Certificate Number 8339.
[24] DOC 4/1/1010 375, and 376. 1904. Abdol Salassa. Mortgage Bond.
[25] MOOC 6/9/7854 74516. 1941. Ismail Mohammad Kasu. Estate Papers.
[26] Voters' Roll 1929. 568 Kasu, Ismail Mahomed Piquetberg Road. Greengrocer Dealer.

sons—Ebrahim (or Braima) and Joseph (or Soppie). The two sons were, therefore, Boeja Joe's second cousins, the sons of his cousin Ameena Salassa. After Ameena Salassa's death, Ismail Mohammad Kasu married Gadeja Brown, and he and Gadeja had four further children—Ayesha, Armina, Fatima, and Sulayman. Either Armina or Fatima was one of the bridesmaids in Mum's wedding photograph.

THE BROWN CONNECTION

The connection between the Salasas and the Browns is a complex one, and has been quite difficult to unravel. This is because Boeja Joe, having been fostered by Gadija Brown when he was young, considered her as "a substitute mother" and her children as "cousins". In fact, it was rumoured that he wanted to marry Gadija's daughter, Auntie Loema, but his parents were against the match, as they were "cousins" and the relationship would have been too close, ignoring the fact that they themselves were first cousins. Auntie Loema never married, and whether this was because she continued to have "feelings" for Bie is not clear. She and Mum became very close friends towards the end of their lives.

I am indebted to Omar Enus and Mr Sulaiman Kasu for clarifying some of the connections between the Salasas and the Browns, according to oral family history. The earliest connection between the two families was in the 1830s, when Abdol Brandt married Soliha, also known as Gasia. Abdol was the son of a Dutchman, and Soliha/Gasia was the daughter of a Bengali father and a French–Creole mother (see above). Abdol and Soliha Brandt had a son, Rajab, born on 20 August 1837, and two daughters. Apparently the two daughters went to live overseas, but Rajab stayed on in the Cape. The Brandt/Brown family are descended from him. When Abdol died, Soliha married Abas Salassa from Malmesbury, from which our side of the family are descended. To put things into perspective, Soliha/Gassia was not only Boeja Joe's grandmother, but also Auntie Loema's great-grandmother. So they were, in fact, second cousins! Soliha/Gassia was a Brandt/Brown by virtue of her first marriage to Abdol Brandt/Brown, and a Salassa when she married Abas Salassa after Abdol died.

RAJAB BRANDT'S FIRST MARRIAGE

Soliha/Gassia's only son, Rajab, married late at the age of 37, a woman 20 years younger, Zana (Zanap?) Angus-Miller, the only child of Shamsuddin and Wagidah Angus-Miller. The couple had five children—Nasterdien, Abdur-Rashid, Gabeebodien Tape, Aisha and Gadija. Zana/Zanap died in 1892 at the age of 35, leaving him with five young children.

Of their five children, Gabiebodien Tape Brown, known to us as "Paatie", married Gadija Waggie (Mème), by whom he had seven children—Janap (Nēnie), Abdul Majiet, Galima (Auntie Loema), Wagied (Tollie), Rajab Tape, Abdulla and Ahmed. Neither of the girls married. Galima, a primary school teacher, taught me at Habibia Primary School. As already mentioned, there had been talk of her marrying Bie, which came to nothing and she remained unmarried to the end of her life.

Rajab Brown, Fatima Kasu, Mum and Kulsum Abrahams, 1942.

Gabiebodien Tape/Paatie died on 6 September 1948,[27] about 10 days before Gadija Salasa. I vaguely remember the funeral from 75 Fenton Road where they lived. His wife, Sis Gadija, was a diminutive soft-spoken lady of great charm. She had a speech defect, which might have been due to a degree of cleft palate. She had fostered Boeja Joe, and after Gadija Salasa died, she became again his "surrogate mother", and "grandmother" to us. She went on the Haj about a year before she died in 1973, a few weeks before Boeja Joe himself died.

---

[27] MMO 6/9/15623 6509/48 1948. Brown, Tape Rajap. Estate Papers.

Their son Rajab Tape was best man at my parents' wedding. He married Moejana Galant from Claremont about a year or two after my parents were married. They were fast friends of my parents to the end of their lives. Rajab Tape was a bricklayer, like my father, and they often worked together on building sites. He was a kind and charming man and, alas, another heavy smoker, and he unfortunately died of cancer of the lungs in the 1980s. Their eldest daughter, Gadija, named after her paternal grandmother, was nearest in age to Saadia, and the two became quite close friends, playing tennis together at the Salt River tennis courts.

ENUS AND KASU

Rajab Brandt's daughter, Gadija, first married Enus Kauchali, by whom she had one child—Mogamat Jaffa Enus (Boeta Jaffa). When Enus Kauchali died, Gadija married Ismail Mohammad Kasu, whose wife, Ameena Salasa, had died and who, as mentioned above, had been the connection between the Kasu and Salasa family. However, Gadija's grandmother and Ameena's grandmother was the same person, namely Soliha/Gassia, so they were in fact second cousins! Gadija had four children—Asa, Armina, Fatima and Sulayman by Ismail Mohammad Kasu.

Boeta Jaffa was a big-built, tall man. He had very strong ideas and was quite active in the building trade union, where he was a kind of shop steward. He was also acutely conscious of his Indian origins—I think his father was from Surat—and this caused him to feel a certain emotional proximity to Mum, whose father came from the Bharuch District, some miles north of Surat, although I do not think they were ever aware of the geography of the area. He scandalised the family at one stage by declaring that he was an Ahmediyya, at a time when the movement was considered to be apostate by the orthodox Muslim clergy. Despite this, the family continued to embrace him, I think in the hope that he would one day "see sense". He further ruffled feathers when he came back from Haj railing against the Saudi exploitation of the pilgrims and, begging Allah's forgiveness, declared that he could never go on Haj again because of this!

RAJAB BRANDT'S SECOND MARRIAGE

Achmat Brown(L) on his return from his second Haj, 1952.

When Rajab Brandt's first wife Zana/ Zanap Angus-Miller died in 1892, he married his second wife, Nahaara Achmat, the only daughter of Imam Hammiem of the Hanafi Mosque,[28] by whom he had several more children, of which only two survived into adulthood —Boeta Achmat Brown and Galima Brown. Boeta Achmat married Safia Karriem, known to us as "Tietie Fiah". They shared the house at 24 Goldsmith Road with Boeja Joe and Mum, shortly after the latter's marriage. The couple had no children of their own, but much later adopted her nephew, Siddique, the son of her sister Zanap Barnes, born Karriem (Amatie). Boeta Achmat was a handsome man. He had a slight stutter. He and Tietie Fiah adopted Siddique around 1948 and the three of them did the Haj together around this time. Boeta Achmat did a second Haj around 1952, this time on his own, and I have a studio photo of him taken on his arrival back.

Boeta Achmat's sister, Galima Brown, married Mogamat Adams, by whom she had five sons—Yusuf (Ta Linkie), Achmat, Ganief (Niefie), Latief (Tiefie) and Rashaad (Saatjie). Their only daughter was Waseela (Siella).

Rajab Brandt/Brown died at the age of 107 on 14 January 1944, in Percy Street, Salt River, behind what is now the Pick and Pay supermarket, but which then was the OK Bazaar, in Lower Main Road, Salt River. His second wife, Nahaara, had predeceased him, having died at the age of 86 in April 1931. On his 100th birthday on 20 August 1937, the *Cape Times*

---

[28] Mosques of the BoKaap, Achmat Davids, Cape Town, Cape and Transvaal Printers (Pty) Ltd, 1980.

published an interview with him in which he reminisces about his life.

From all of this, it is clear that there is a link between the Salasas and the Browns. Auntie Loema's paternal great-grandmother, Soliha/Gassia, is also Boeja Joe's paternal grandmother. Soliha's son, Rajab Brandt, and Saban Salasa were half-brothers.

The Brandt family changed their name in the early 20th century to Brown. The Salassas also changed the spelling of their family name to Salasa in the middle of the 20th century.

ABAS AND SOLIHA/GASSIA SALASSA

There is a document in the Cape Town Archives dated May 1879[29] about an Abdol Salassa, a painter, living in Paarl, who was convicted in the Supreme Court for "Assault with Intent to do Grievous Bodily Harm". He was sentenced to receive 50 lashes and two years' hard labour. He would have completed his sentence by May or June 1881, and if on his release from prison he kept out of trouble, he may well have been able to rehabilitate himself to the extent of being able to take out a mortgage on a property in Malmesbury in 1899, hence the mortgage bond of that date in the name of Abdol Salasa mentioned earlier. I strongly suspect that he might well be Abas's third son, Abdol, whose daughter Ameena married Ismail Kasu.

Abas and Soliha also had three daughters that we know of—Sabbreya (or Sabria), who I have already mentioned, and about whom we know very little, Asa van Witt and Francina Georgina Julison. Asa van Witt was born in Malmesbury around 1884. We know little about her early life, but she was known to Boeja Joe, who was a teenager when she died. Her death notice[30] states that her parents were Abas and Gasia. It states that her husband was a mason and that he died around 1933, but other than that there is no more known about him. They had no children. She died on

---

[29] CSC 1/1/1/27 1 1879. The Queen vs Abdol Salasa.
[30] MOOC 6/9/4834 52166 1936 Van Witt, Asa, née Salassa. Estate Papers.

16 October 1936 at her home at 26 Goldsmith Road just three years after her husband. She had made a will on 20 September 1936, less than a month before her death, bequeathing everything she owned to her "one and only brother, Saban Salasa". Interestingly, one of the witnesses to the will was her nephew, Karriem Salasa! I have been unable to find her husband's death notice so far. Oral family history has it that she actually died at 28 Goldsmith Road in what was my bedroom, but there is now no one alive who can confirm this.

Abas and Gassia's third daughter was Francina Georgina Julison, born Salasa. Again, there is little known about her early life and her marriage. Her death notice[31] states that she born in Malmesbury. She was 60 years old when she died on 22 September 1930 at her home at 26 Goldsmith Road, which puts her date of birth as 1870 and means that she was about 16 years older than her brother, Saban, and about 14 years older than her sister, Asa. Her husband was a Frederick Augustus Julison, who died on 10 July 1930,[32] only two months before her own death. His occupation is given as a carpenter, and they must have lived in Chapel Street, Woodstock, as this is given as the address where he died. (By a strange coincidence, Rush teaches at the primary school in Chapel Street!) He was 10 years her senior and they had no children. Intriguingly, there is a court record in the Cape Town Archives, dated 1898, that cites him seeking a divorce from his wife, Johanna Catherina Sara Julison.[33] This would be more than 30 years before Francina's and his own death in 1930. It is pure speculation whether he divorced his wife to marry Francina!

She had also made a will about a month before she died. It states that when making the will she was "lying seriously ill" at 26 Goldsmith Road. She had a little money in the African Homes

[31] MOOC 6/9/3773 27732 1930 Julison, Francina Georgina née Salasa. Estate Papers.
[32] MOOC 6/9/3731 26831 1930 Julison, Frederick Augustus. Estate Papers.
[33] CSC 2/1/1/351 157 Illiquid Case. Frederick Augustus Julison vs Johanna Catherina Sara Julison, born Sullivan. Action for Dissolution of the Bonds of Marriage, 1898.

Trust, which she left to her sister, Asa van Witt, to be used to pay for her funeral. There should be records of her funeral and burial in one of the churches in Salt River, Cape Town. Oral family history is that when she died, Saban and Gadija did not know if it would be possible as devout Muslims to bury her as a Christian, and they consulted the Sheikh at the Azzavia Mosque, which they attended, as to their dilemma. The Sheikh apparently reassured them that according to Islamic law they could bury Saban's sister according to her religion. This implies that she had either in the past converted to Christianity or that she was born a Christian. The romantic in me suspects that she may well have converted to Christianity in order to marry her husband, Frederick.

It seems that of all Abas's children, only Saban, Abdol and Sabria had any issue. As far as we know, Abdol had only one child, Ameena, mentioned above, while Sabria had two children, Abdol Karriem and Gassia. As Saban was the only one with male issue, the Salasas descend from his line.

SABAN AND GADIJA SALASSA'S CHILDREN

Saban and Gadija had 11 children. Their births were carefully recorded in a little red notebook, which I still have, giving the date of birth in the Gregorian calendar and sometimes in the Hijri calendar. The eldest child, Amena, born on 7 August 1905, died within months of her birth.

GALIELA SALAAM, born SALASA

The second child, also a daughter, Galiela, was born on 21 June 1907. As Saban and Gadija were newly married at this time, it is possible that Galiela was born either in Malmesbury or possibly in District Six, if the newlyweds had already moved to Cape Town by then. Her

Galiela Salaam, born Salasa, circa 1969.

early life was not spoken about much and I don't recall her ever talking about it herself. She was known to the family as "Tietie".[34] She married Ismail Salaam and they had 10 children surviving into adulthood. Oral family history has it that Galiela married when she was about 16 or 17 years old. She was short in stature, like her mother, Gadija. She too was fair in complexion but had brown eyes. She was quite aware of her position as the eldest of Saban's surviving children and expected to be treated as such. When her mother, Gadija, died in 1948, she took her role as the eldest surviving daughter seriously and considered herself to be the surrogate mother of the family. She had a hearty laugh and enjoyed a joke. In fact, she often laughed so heartily that she wet herself. Only years later, when I qualified as a doctor, did I realise that she must have had stress incontinence due to her many pregnancies. She was very generous to the children of the family and one could look forward to always having a threepenny piece or sixpence stuffed into your hand when you met her!

She was always veiled when she left her house and would disapprove violently of women who weren't. She felt it her duty to be critical of what she considered to be "lax practices" so as not to disgrace the family.

Boeja Joe, Hadjie Ismail Salaam and Uncle Allie Salasa.

Hadjie Ismail Salaam was a tailor by trade, who had a shop on the Lower Main Road in Woodstock. The family lived in Devon Street, Woodstock, a street away from the shop, although they may well have lived in the Bo-Kaap before then, or even in District Six. The 1929 Voters Roll lists Hadjie Abdol Salaam as a joint tenant living at 124 Church Street. Also living there was

---

[34] *Tietie* is a word of unknown origin used by the Cape Malays to mean an older sister.

Hadjie Ismail Salaam. Both are listed as tailors. There is a document in the Cape Town Archives referring to a Slum Clearance Act that mentions Hadjie Abdol Salaam, Hadjie Ismail's father.[35]

In 1929 Galiela would have been about 22 years old and she and Hadjie Ismail would probably have been married for about five or six years, with possibly one or more young children. Living with one's parents-in-law in an extended family was not unusual in those days, until a couple could afford a place of their own, but conditions at 124 Church Street must have been very cramped, hence the difficulty with the Slum Clearance Act. It is not clear when the family moved to the house in Devon Street, Woodstock, but in comparison it must have seemed like a palace!

For some years when I was little, Hadjie Ismail used to make my Eid suit! His family had been in the tailoring business for some years and all his daughters left school early to learn the trade, as apprentices, from their father. When they were considered to have acquired enough skill as seamstresses, they were allowed to work in one of the local clothing factories. The boys were encouraged to continue schooling for as long as they could.

Hadjie Ismail was a devout man and often conducted the family prayers at weddings, naming ceremonies, funerals and other occasions, when the Sheikh from the Azzavia was not available. He was about 5ft 10in in height and always well dressed in a suit, as befitted a tailor, when he went out. He wore a fez with a black tassel, in those days indicating that he had been on the Haj. This custom died out in the late 20th century. At home he wore a white *jellabia* or *thawb*. He was very dark in complexion and never readily smiled, so that as children we were always a little frightened and in awe of him. In fact, he and Galiela were very strict disciplinarians with their own children. The couple had 10 children surviving into adulthood—Salega, Ayesha, Mymona, Rachmat, Zubeida, Safia, Jameel, AbdulAziz, Salim and Shafiq. It is pure speculation, but it is possible that Salega was named after Galiela's grandmother, Soliha/Gassia. To me the names are similar

---

[35] KAB 3/CT 4/1/5/1101 L257/5 Slums Act 53 of 1936. No 124 Church Street. Abdol Salaam.

enough to be interchangeable. Galiela died in early 1969, a few months after performing her Haj. Hadjie Ismail never remarried and died on 18 August 1978.[36]

Salega was the eldest of the Salaam children and was only a few years younger than my mother. She was the tallest of the girls in her family and fair in complexion like her mother. She was courted by an older man, Hadjie Abdulla Gabier, whom her parents disapproved of for some years; but eventually they relented and the couple were married. I have no idea what the reason for their opposition was, apart from the age difference, but the couple were determined to have their parents' approval to marry, and as a result, Salega saw three of her younger sisters married before her, at a time when there was a strict chronological order for siblings to be married. In fact, they became the "Romeo and Juliette" figures of the family! They had two children—Nazlie and Nasief. Salega too had the familial diseases—diabetes, high blood pressure and heart disease—and died of a heart attack.

The second daughter in the family was Ayesha. She too was fair and tall. She married Ghidr Parker, one of the famous Parker family and patrons of Habibia. They had only one child, a son, Ismail, named after his maternal grandfather. Ayesha, in later life, had diabetes and developed gangrene in one of her legs, which had to be amputated.

The third daughter was Mymona (or Moena as she was nicknamed). She was dark in complexion like her father. She married Ghoesain Abdurahman. Her daughter, Nazli, married Moena's cousin, Achmat Salasa (see below). After her marriage, Moena lived with her younger married sister, Rachmat, in Greatmore Street, Woodstock, around the corner from her father's tailor shop. In later life she also contracted the family disease of diabetes and became blind because of diabetic retinopathy.

Rachmat (or Ragmie) was the first of the Salaam girls to get married. She had a vibrant personality and a sense of humour perhaps only rivalled by Boeja Joe with whom she had a good

---

[36] Death Notice No 7445 Hadjie Ismail Salaam. Died 18 August 1978.

rapport. She married Ebrahim (Braima) Ganief, by whom she had three children—Safwaan, Talib and Ismail (the latter named after his maternal grandfather).

Saban and Gadija's next child, Ahmed, born on 5 July 1909, died after a few months.

SHARIEFA CORNELIUS, formerly ABRAHAMS, born SALASA

Their next child, Shariefa (Riefa), was born on 7 April 1911. Riefa was a tall woman, about 6ft in height, like her father, from whom she must have inherited the gene for tallness, and which she passed on to the children from her first marriage. We called her "Auntie", so Saadia and I had two "Aunties"—Riefa and Mum's sister, Gall! Riefa was fair in complexion, like her mother and elder sister, with brown eyes. She married Armien Abrahams, by whom she had four children—Gadija (Dija), Farieda, Ebrahim (Hiema) and Mariam (Poppy). Armien Abrahams was apparently very fair and very tall with reddish hair, according to oral family history, and from a family who very probably had recent White blood added to their gene pool. He apparently fell ill, probably with tuberculosis, shortly after he married, and died in 1943 when his youngest daughter, Poppy, was only a few months old. Riefa was left with a young family to care for on her own. At the time, they had been living at either 24 or 26 Goldsmith Road, from where she and the children moved to 28 Goldsmith Road to live with her parents, where she lived until Saban died in 1955. She remarried around 1954 to the widower, Imam Allie Cornelius of Constantia, whose wife had recently died. Imam Allie Cornelius had several grown-up children by his first marriage, some of whom were living with him. He and Riefa had one child together,

Shariefa Cornelius, born Salasa, at her youngest son, Shadley's, wedding, circa 1979.

Mohamad Shadley, who is about the same age as Rush. They separated shortly after, and she and the children returned to live with her widower father, Saban, at 28 Goldsmith Road.

Riefa's eldest daughter, Gadija (or Dija), named after her maternal grandmother, Gadija Salasa, left school early to work in order to support the family. She had several factory jobs, but memorably, one at a hat factory in Coleridge Road. She became so proficient at it that she set up a small sideline doing hats at home and selling them at cut price! Working at the same factory was the wife of a cricketer who left South Africa for England, as there were no opportunities for non-White players in the racist game in South Africa. Presently, he was selected for the England team! His name? Basil D'Oliveira! He made the newspapers when he was chosen by the England captain to play in the team about to tour South Africa. When the racists saw the list of players, they refused to give D'Oliveira a visa, and ignominiously for the English team, the captain de-selected him so that the tour could go ahead. Such were the lengths people went to in order to appease the racists. Dija loved children and was always first to visit the newborns in the family. When Fow was born, she particularly took to her, and that bond remained until she died on 29 March 2007.

Farieda, Riefa's second daughter, also left school early, to work in a cigarette factory, making Cavalla cigarettes, then a very popular local brand. The workers were allowed to keep any misshapen or damaged cigarettes for themselves but often sold them on to supplement their meagre wages. She later worked in a sweet factory where the same principle applied, and as a result, all our teeth were riddled with dental caries after eating so much sugar! Dija married an aged widower, who died a matter of months after the marriage. They had no children of their own, although he had grown-up married children from his first marriage. She died in 2007. Farieda never married. Both Dija and Farieda were tall, more than 6ft in height. Dija was dark in complexion, whereas the other three were fair, apparently like their father's family.

Shariefa's only son by Armien Abrahams was Ebrahim Abrahams, nicknamed "Hiema". He is tall, at 6ft 1in, and fair, like the rest of his family. He too left school early to work, at first in a laundry in Junction Road, Salt River, and latterly with one of the big oil companies, where he stayed until his retirement. He first married a girl, Farieda. I was best man at the wedding, which was a big affair at the Maitland Town Hall. The *bruidskamer* (literally, bride's room) was at 28 Goldsmith Road. Unfortunately, the marriage lasted only a few weeks. He remarried to Faldeela Parker, by whom he has several children.

The youngest of Shariefa's daughters, Mariam, also known as Poppy, fell pregnant in her late teens by a man who left her. As abortion was illegal and unheard of at the time, she had the baby, Gatiem. Riefa and her two older daughters, Dija and Farieda practically brought Gatiem up as their own, and there is still a very strong bond of affection between them all. When Gatiem was in his teens, and after Rifa's death, Poppy married Faiz Toefy, a relation of the Azzavia Sheikhs, but he died tragically of cancer of the lungs and she was left a widow before she was 50. They had a son called Yagyah.

BOEJA JOE/BIE/YUSUF SALASA

Saban and Gadija's eldest surviving son was my father, Boeja Joe. As I mentioned before, he was named after Gadija's father, Joseph Stephanus.

When the racist government introduced the identity card system around 1950, it became compulsory for everyone to carry an identity card showing their identity number, their racial category and a passport-sized photo. Before this time, only Africans had been compelled to carry the infamous passbook, which gave details of their domicile, their place of birth and work, apart from the identity number. These had to be scrupulously updated at every change of residence and work, and failure to do so would result in severe punishments, including prison. All the other racial groups, with the exception of the Whites, were violently opposed to the system being extended to them, knowing how harshly the government enforced the Pass Laws on the African population and fearing that the dreaded identity card would be used against them in the same way to control the freedom of movement of the population. It was also feared that it was a way of enforcing the Group Areas Act, intended to keep the races apart and confined to their respective racially segregated residential areas. It was indeed part of a master plan to segregate everyone on the grounds of race, which the government euphemistically called "Separate Parallel Development" or "Apartheid".

Boeja Joe/Bie/Yusuf Salasa, identity card photo, circa 1950.

In order to apply for the appropriate identity card, one had to provide, apart from the passport-sized photo, a copy of one's birth certificate, and Boeja Joe took this opportunity of changing his name on his birth certificate to "Yusuf", the Arabic equivalent of Joseph. I think he wanted the change to make sure that his name would not be a barrier to his race being doubted, in that he was a Cape Malay, and not Coloured. If there had been confusion, he would, by the new Group Areas Act, which set aside separate residential areas for the different races, have had to reside in a Coloured area away from those of his family with more overtly Arabic names, who would have had to live in the Malay area.

In a similar vein, Mum had been classified as Indian, and although my parents had had a civil marriage before their traditional Muslim wedding, there was bureaucratic confusion as to Saadia and my racial category. We were clearly not Cape Malay or Indian, and according to the Race Classification Act would have had to have been described as Mixed. I think both my parents, like many other families in similar situations, were afraid of the consequences of all these laws being rigidly implemented. On paper it looked as if my parents would have to split up, with Mum living in an Indian area, possibly in Grahamstown with her parents—for there would be no point in her remaining in Cape Town—and Boeja Joe living in the Cape Malay area of Cape

Town. Where Saadia and I would live in this scheme of things was uncertain! Although these fears were very real at the time, thankfully things turned out differently. Mum's identity card, and the Book of Life that subsequently replaced it, continued to show her as being racially Indian.

Boeja Joe was known as either "Joe" or "Joesy" to the end of his life. He was about 5ft 10 or 11in and of a muscular build. He was olive complexioned with square features, and as is evident from his photos, quite handsome. He was gentle in manner and always the joker in the family, and the life and soul of any gathering. Family and friends loved his stories and he was sought after at weddings for his *bruids liedjies* (wedding songs) about a tree and its branches, which could go on for almost half an hour or longer if his audience so wished it, with him improvising all the time on the theme!

With Saadia and me he was gentle and loving, although she was

Yusuf /Joseph Salasa, circa 1972.

Saban and Gadija's four sons—AbuBakr (Kaatjie), Yusuf (Boeja Joe), Allie and Osman (seated), circa 1940.

obviously the apple of his eye. He indulged us almost to the point of spoiling us. He had a good repertoire of stories about a fictional character called Juha, who I later discovered exists in *One Thousand and One Nights*! Although Boeja Joe read the newspapers, I only saw him read thrillers rather than anything more serious, so how he came to know these stories from *One Thousand and One Nights* I don't know. He was fond of the *News of the World*, which we got every week as soon as the mail ship from Southampton docked in Cape Town on a

Wednesday. Even then, the paper was already two weeks out of date! He loved to browse around second-hand bookshops, and would indulge this pleasure on a Saturday morning at the flea market on the Grand Parade in front of the Cape Town City Hall, often coming back with a battered old second-hand copy of a Dick Cheney thriller.

In those days everyone would wear red fezzes, but Boeja Joe often wore a grey Trilby felt hat when seeing friends on a Saturday afternoon. He always wore his fez at a jaunty angle, as he does in his identity card photo. The fez gradually became replaced by the skull cap in the 1960s, and in later photos he is seen mostly wearing this. He was a dapper dresser, always well turned out for family occasions or even just for the visiting round on a Sunday afternoon, when everyone visited each other for a chat and a cup of tea. He was not easily roused to anger, but when we did try his patience, he could flare up. However, his temper subsided as quickly and he would almost be remorseful after a flare up, as if in apology for his loss of control. He never hit me in all my life and only once made as if to hit Saadia when she was a teenager after some trivial argument. She was so shocked at the threat that she burst out crying, but surprisingly and amusingly, he cried with her in remorse.

There is a gap of about two and a half years between me and Saadia, but some seven years between her and Rush. Mum and Boeja Joe had prepared Saadia and me for Rush's birth, so we knew more or less when the birth was expected and were involved in getting the layettes together for the new baby. For some reason Rush called Boeja Joe "Bie", and so we all took to calling him by that name. Fow was born about seven years after Rush. Bie died quite unexpectedly of a heart attack on 3 August 1973.[37] He had lived to see me graduate as a doctor from the University of Cape Town in December 1967. In the summer of 1972, I had obtained a Diploma in Psychological Medicine (DPM) from the Royal Colleges of Physicians and Surgeons in England. The *Cape Times*

---

[37] Death Certificate No B199325.

reported the event in a short article, noting that of only three candidates from South Africa who had obtained the degree that year, I was the first and only non-White to receive it. We found the clipping in his wallet after his death. He must have been proud of the achievement to have carried it around with him all the time. He had performed his Haj about a year before his death.

BOETA ALLIE'S FAMILY

Saban and Gadija's second eldest son, Allie, was born on 19 April 1923. Boeta Allie was fair in complexion like his mother and was about 5ft 10in in height. He had greenish eyes and had a tendency to put on weight, so I nicknamed him "Fat Uncle". He enjoyed his food, and when warned about the family history of high blood pressure, diabetes and heart disease, he would always say that it was not the time yet to start worrying about it. He, like Bie, had a good sense of humour. Unlike the rest of the family, he had a tendency to thriftiness. He married Mariam Perrin in March 1945, about a week after Saadia was born.

Auntie Mariam's father, Chacha[38] Cassiem, a Gujarati man from Surat, had a general dealer's business in Kensington. Her mother, whose name was Fatima, also known as "Sis Tiemie", was a Toefy, and said to be related to the Sheikhs at the Azzavia Mosque. Chacha Cassiem had been married in India before he came to South Africa, but had lost touch with his Indian wife and children. Many years later, in the late 1950s, he had a severe heart attack and was not expected to live. He became very depressed and guilty about the family he had lost touch with in India, and when he learnt that I had traced Mum's relations in India, he asked me to do the same for him. This was difficult, as South Africa had no diplomatic relations with India and the nearest Indian Embassy was in Nairobi. However, I was delighted when they replied in a relatively short time with the name and address of his eldest son. I wrote to him on behalf of Chacha Cassiem and

---

[38] *Chacha* is the Urdu word for uncle.

they were able to make contact, and subsequently Chacha Cassiem was able to go to India on a visit, accompanied by his youngest daughter, Amina. He died shortly after returning to South Africa.

Auntie Mariam was short in stature and dark in complexion. She had a remarkable memory and kept the genealogies of many of the local families in her head. She could recount the dark secrets of practically everyone in the family. She would have been invaluable in compiling this record! The familial illnesses of diabetes and heart disease finally caught up with Boeta Allie, in spite of his sanguine attitude towards them, and he died of a heart attack on 3 April 1979.[39] Auntie Mariam had throughout her life suffered from "a delicate stomach" and died of cancer of the stomach.[40]

The couple had four children—Lutfiah, Mohamed Faiz, Gadija and Fadiela. When they were little, I babysat them while their parents and mine went to the cinema on a Saturday evening. Lutfiah, the eldest daughter, married Ganief Israil around 1968, shortly after I left South Africa for exile in London. They have three children—Zaida, Lamees and Zaid. Zaida married Riyaad Gydien and has two children—Zaina and Thania.

Mohamed Faiz, the only son, married Faika, who converted to Islam on their marriage, and they have four children— Ghairunissa, Shahnaz, Ghoesain and Camita. Ghairunissa married Ebrahim Essa and has four children—Faisal, Feriaal, Elyaas and Mikaeel. He married a second time around 2001, to Shaheeda Manuel, and has a son, Muhammad Zubayr, by her.

Gadija, the second daughter, named after her paternal grandmother, Gadija Salasa, married Ismail Emandien, by whom she had four children—Zahir, Rhoda, Ilhaam and Somayah. Gadija died tragically of a stroke due to high blood pressure when their children were still under the age of 10. They were raised by their father, Ismail. The eldest, Zahir, married Rameeza Madjal and has three children—Sufiaan, Malika and Shakier. Their elder daughter, Rhoda, married Waleed Wilson, and has two children— Imraan and Waseem. The next eldest, Ilhaam, married Shamiel

---

[39] Death Certificate Number 2357.
[40]

Dollie, by whom she has a son, Irshaad. The youngest, Sumaya, married Zahier Samuels, and they do not have any children as yet.

MARIAM DAVIDS, born SALASA, "GALATIE"

Saban and Gadija's next child was a girl named Mariam, born on 19 November 1920. We called her "Galatie"[41] but her peers nicknamed her "Mattie". She was short, about 5ft 7in, dark in complexion and, like her brother Allie, had a tendency to put on weight. I have a studio photo of her taken around 1943, showing a very elegant and beautiful young woman smiling confidently at the camera. She is unveiled and wearing only a headscarf elegantly draped over her head. Galatie was always a

Mariam Davids, born Salasa, circa 1943.

great favourite with the children, and I suppose because she was our youngest aunt we were less in awe of her than we were of the other two. One felt one could have a laugh and a joke with her. She was a good cook, but her *koeksisters* were to die for! They were rich and she always stuffed them with coconut. She must have passed on the recipe to her eldest daughter, Gadija, who makes them well too, but not quite like her mother!

She married Mohamad Darawish Davids (or "Dallie" as he became known), the son of Imam Mouliat Davids. The latter had been imam in Kimberly, where he and his wife, Fatima, had their three children, Mohamad Salie, Mohamad Darawish, and the only girl, Mahdia. Fatima's maiden name was apparently Joseph, and through that line she was related to both the Scello and the Abrahams families. The family moved to Cape Town, where shortly after, Imam Davids died, leaving Mohamad Darawish to

---

[41] From the Arabic *Gal*, meaning maternal aunt. Literally, "my maternal aunt".

look after his mother and sister; so when Galatie married him, she had to live with her mother-in-law and sister-in-law, a very strained relationship which remained so until they both died.

Boeta Dallie's mother, Fatima, developed Parkinson's disease in the middle of the 1960s and became bedridden and demented towards the end. In the final stages of the disease, she was unable to speak or indeed to swallow and needed full nursing care, and because Mahdia was unable to cope, the burden fell on Galatie. She died on 6 June 1979.[42]

Mahdia was a seamstress and suffered from severe asthma attacks, often set off by the dust and cotton fibres from her sewing, and was, therefore, unable to work a lot of the time. With an aged mother, and with her unable to work to support the two of them, the task fell to Dallie and Galatie. Mahdia was very fair in complexion, with blond hair and blue eyes, very much like her elder brother, Salie, in contrast to Dallie who was very dark in complexion. She had a constant asthmatic wheeze, which made it difficult for her to speak without becoming out of breath, but she bore her illness with great fortitude. She died a spinster, although it was rumoured that in her youth she had had many suitors.

Dallie was a character with a sense of humour that some found irritating at times. He was devoted to Galatie, calling her "Sweets", and would talk openly, even in front of us children, about how good their sex life was, at a time when talking about sex was still a taboo. I think he did this just to be provocative and to tease Galatie. Dallie had a heart attack around 1966 but made a good recovery and died almost 20 years later on 6 February 1982.[43] Galatie died almost exactly a year later on 8 February 1983 in Medina, while on the Haj.[44]

They had five children, of whom four survived into adulthood. The eldest, Fatima, died of pneumonia on 24 October 1948,[45] at the age of four months, just over a month after her maternal

---

[42] Death Certificate Number 3683.
[43] Death Certificate Number 3684.
[44] Death Certificate Number 1026.
[45] Death Certificate Number 3744.

grandmother, Gadija, died. She had been named after her paternal grandmother, Fatima Davids. Galatie and Dallie were renting a room with us at 59 Fenton Road at the time.

Their eldest son was Mohamad Salie, who was deaf and dumb and was sent to a special school for the deaf and dumb at Wittebome. He got on well and learnt to sign, and also to speak after a fashion. While at the special school, he met a girl, Latiefa, with similar problems, whom he subsequently married, despite his parents' fear that a marriage between two such disabled people would produce offspring who were also disabled. However, they have had three girls—Zuraida, Fatima and Mariam (the latter two named, respectively, after his paternal grandmother, Fatima Davids, and his mother, Galatie). Despite the fears, I have not heard that any of them are disabled. Mohamad Salie was the fairest of Galatie's children, with blue-green eyes.

Galatie and Boeta Dallie next had a daughter, Gadija, named after Galatie's mother. Gadija trained as a nurse and rose to become a nursing sister. She is a loving and very caring person, as shown by her choice of profession. She married Mohamad Tape Jassiem and bore him three children—Shamiel, Shamiela and Mahdi.

After Gadija, the second son, Yusuf, was born, named after Boeja Joe, who Galatie was very fond of. Yusuf was dark in complexion, like his father, and a bit of a wild one. He married a very sensible girl, Aziza, by whom he had three children. The eldest, Mohamed Hassan, was born prematurely. Aziza had gone into labour unexpectedly and Galatie, in great anxiety, because no midwife could be found, asked me to come and "have a look", as we lived just around the corner from them. I was a fourth-year medical student at the time and had just completed my obstetrics and gynaecology. I arrived to find the child about to be born and had no alternative but to deliver him myself, regardless of the consequences. He was so small that he could fit into a shoebox! At Galatie and Dallie's behest, he was named Mohamed Hassan after me. They had two further children—Darawish (named after his father) and Mymona. Yusuf died tragically in a motor car accident in 1982/3.

Galatie's next daughter was Mymona (or "Monie"). She married Dawood Behardien. Monie is dark in complexion, and in looks very much resembles her mother. She has four children—Mohamad Amin, Achmat, Anees and Adnaan. Monie became a care assistant working with the elderly. She worked for a while in a home for the elderly in the UK, where she was very well thought of for her caring attitude towards her patients and for her organising ability.

The youngest of Galatie's children is Benjamien, married to Faiza, by whom he has four children—Amina, Mariam, Magmoed and Ridwaan.

BOETA KAATJIE – ABUBAKR SALASA

AbuBakr (Boeta Kagee) and Rokaya Kriel, 24 April 1948.

Saban and Gadija next had a son called AbuBakr, nicknamed "Kaatjie", born on 16 September 1926. Boeta Kaatjie was tall, about 5ft 11in, always slim, and fair in complexion, like his mother. He was soft spoken and gentle. Unlike his other brothers, he was physically slight. He was quite artistic and creative. I don't know the reason why he did not follow his father and brothers into the building trade, but I suspect it was because he was rather delicate and not in robust health as a youth. He always had a bit of an artistic streak, which in those days attracted derogatory comments about artistic people being workshy.

He married Rokaya Kriel, the niece of his cousin Karriem Salasa's wife. Rokaya was Rachmat Kriel's brother's daughter. The wedding was on 24 April 1948, just five months before his mother, Gadija Salasa, passed away. Rokaya Kriel was born on 31 May 1926. I remember their wedding well.

The reception was held at Wellington House (20 Goldsmith Road), to keep 28 Goldsmith Road free for the *bruidskamer* (bridal chamber). Rokaya's family lived in Paarl, so the traditional exchange of visits of the bridal couple between their separate receptions, where family and friends could see the new additions to the family, could not take place because of the distance involved between Paarl and Salt River. Boeta Kaatjie made his wedding cake himself, and decorated it, working the icing into garlands and flowers. It was a sight to behold and led people who saw it to commission wedding cakes from him, and it became something of a profession for him. He had also created all the table decorations and the festive banners that decorated his wedding reception, and had been actively involved in the furnishings of the bridal chamber.

Boeta Kaatjie and Rokaya had seven children—Nadeema, Achmat, Rhoda, Yusuf, Nurunissa, Ashraf and Shuaib.

Nadeema married Faisal Kasu, whose grandfather, Ismail Mohammad Kasu, had married Boeta Kaatjie's cousin, Ameena Salassa/Abdol (see above under "The Brown—Kasu Connection"). Faisal's mother, Auntie Kulsum, was born Abrahams, the sister of Armien Abrahams, Auntie Riefa's (Sharifa Salasa's) first husband. These marriages, therefore, linked the Abrahams, Kasu, Kriel and Salasa families. Auntie Kulsum is also the second bridesmaid in Mum's wedding photo! Faisal was a teacher and later became headmaster of his school until he retired from teaching. The couple have three children—Natheer, Faika and Yazeed.

Achmat married his second cousin, Nazli Abdurahman, his aunt, Galiela Salaam's granddaughter. They have three children—Rokaya (named after his mother) Mymona (named after her mother) and AbuBakr (named after his father).

Rhoda married Dr Rafiq Darsi, but the marriage did not work out and they divorced after having one child, Shafika. She remarried someone from Durban.

Yusuf (named after my father) married Farieda Soeker, and the couple have four children—Kamal, Mawadda, Achmat and Hishaam. Farieda teaches at the same school as Rush, Chapel Street Primary School in Woodstock, where Fow also taught for a short time, so at one time there were three Salasas teaching at the same school!

Nurunissa married Majdi Jackson.

Ashraf married Mariam Kammies. There may be a link, as yet unexplored, between her family and the Salasas (see Kammies Salassa below), which needs further exploration.

Shuaib married Nazeema.

Boeta Kaatjie was diagnosed with having pulmonary tuberculosis when the first four of his children were literally babes in arms. In those days the newer anti-tubercular drugs had not yet been discovered, so the diagnosis was a serious one. He had to have one lung removed surgically and was admitted to the TB isolation unit at Conradie Hospital, where he was an inpatient for the best part of a year. Bie and Mum took on the task of supporting the family, for which they were always grateful and which forged a link between them for the rest of their lives. I suspect it was as a result of this that they named their fourth child, Yusuf, after my father.

When he was declared as "no longer infectious" we were allowed to visit him in hospital and I was amazed at the range of occupational therapy options that there were for the patients, so much so that I almost wished that I could be hospitalised! Boeta Kaatjie was taught many skills in the occupational therapy department, from which he would be able to make a living when he left hospital. He lived a reasonably healthy life after this traumatic episode, and in contrast to his three brothers, who all died before the age of 60, he lived on until he was 70. He died on 16 November 1996, after a heart attack.

Boeta Kaatjie and his wife, Rogaya, along with his sister, Galatie, and Mum went on their first Haj in 1983. Women cannot undertake the Haj travelling on their own and have to be accompanied by their husbands or a male relative. As Mum and Galatie were both widows, Boeta Kaatjie acted as their male relative. Rather tragically, Galatie died in Medina on her visit to the Prophet's tomb.

On her 80th birthday, in 2006, Boeta Kaatjie's widow, Rogaya, was entertained to a huge family gathering consisting of all her surviving brothers and sisters, her children and their spouses, and her grandchildren. A commemorative DVD of the occasion was compiled by her children with help from all the family, tracing her Kriel ancestors and important events in her early and married life, with accompanying photos from their archives. I was pleasantly surprised, when I saw it some years later, to see a photo taken in Johannesburg of the group, including Mum and Galatie, when they were stopping over on their way to Saudi Arabia. It was probably the last photo taken of Galatie, who died a few days later in Medina.

OSMAN SALASA - BOETA OESSIE

The youngest of Saban and Gadija's children was Osman, born on 23 December 1928. "Boeta Oessie", as we knew him, was a shy young man always keeping in the background. He was olive complexioned and about 5ft 10in in height. A bricklayer, like his brothers, he worked with them for most of his life. As the youngest in the family, he was only 19 when his mother died in September 1948. He never talked of the trauma of his mother's death at such an early age.

He married Fatima Dreyer, born on 15 January 1929, on the 2 February 1952. Her mother, Jobaida, born Rayland, had died on 24 October 1951,[46] four months before their marriage. She would have had to live alone after her mother's death, at 100 Aspeling Street, District Six, as her elder sister, Farieda, was married and living with her own in-laws, the Mosavels, in Black River. I suspect that this was the reason for the marriage taking place so soon after her mother's death. Farieda was Fatima's half-sister, born of the same mother but different fathers. Like Fatima, she was very fair and beautiful, but in a different way to her sister.

---

[46] MOOC 6/9/19022 6907/51. 1951. Kamaar, Jobaida or Bayra, formerly Dreyer, née Rayland. Estate Papers.

Farieda divorced her husband in 1958[47] and died of cancer in the 1970s.

At the time of Boeta Oessie's marriage, Galatie and Boeta Dallie were living with Boeja Joe and Mum in a two-bedroom house at 59 Fenton Road, which meant that each family, with two children each, had one bedroom. As the newly wedded Boeta Oessie and Fatima would be living at 28 Goldsmith Road with Saban (as tradition dictated), it was agreed that Galatie and Boeta Dallie would move into Fatima's family home in Aspeling Street, which eased the housing situation all round.

Fatima was an extremely beautiful young woman, very fair in complexion and perhaps as tall as her husband, as evidenced by their wedding photo, which still survives. The couple had six children, five of them surviving into adulthood. All of their children were fair in complexion and around their parents' height when they grew into adulthood. The youngest child was stillborn.

The eldest, Mohamad Faiz, was born on 8 September 1953, making him just about a year older than Rush. He married Zogera Magiet, born on 28 December 1955, and they have three children—Riyaad, Rizwaan and Rushana.

Riyaad married Nawaal Isaacs and the couple have two children—Shaheed and Zubaida (the latter named for his maternal grandmother). Unfortunately, this marriage did not work out. He remarried in 2005 to Gouwah Soloman, by whom he has two further children—Mogammad Faaiz (named after his father) and Ismail (named after her father). She has two daughters by a previous marriage—Afaaf and Huda Hendricks.

Rizwaan was born on 23 September 1977 and married Khairunissa Dollie, born on 3 January 1977. They have a daughter, Hannah, born on 3 July 2003.

Boeta Oessie's second son, Abdul Haadi, was born on 26 January 1955. He married Narrima Martin, born on 27 November 1959, and they have three children—Yazeed (born on 21 July

---

[47] CSC 2/1/1/1991 551 1958. Illiquid cases. Restitution of Conjugal Rights. Fareeda Mosavel, born Kamaar vs Karriem Mosavel.

1976), Rushda (born on 1 November 1980) and Umayma (born on 9 May 1986).

Boeta Oessie's third son, AbdulNasir, married Faiza Davids, born on 13 July 1957, and this couple have four children—Hafiz (born on 2 June 1979), Luqman (born on 19 September 1986), Niamat (born on 4 January 1988) and Uthman (born on 21 March 1992), who was probably named for his paternal grandfather. Hafiz married Zahieda Gallow, born on 24 September 1980. They have two children—Mohammad Amaar and Hannia. I am very indebted to AbdulNasir, who gathered all the details of his side of the family for me when he heard that I was building up a record.

Boeta Oessie's only daughter, Widaad, married Faghmie Soloman, born on 5 June 1964, and the couple have three children—Ziyaad (born on 17 July 1988), Zaahid (born on 13 May 1993) and Sitaara (born on 7 October 1999).

His youngest son, Mogamat Mahdi, was born on 19 March 1960, which makes him a few months older than Fow. Thus, all of Boeta Oessie's children were born during the six years that separated Rush and Fow's birth. Mogamat Mahdi married Fatima Abrahams, born on 29 December 1963, and they have two children—Naweed (born on 21 December 1990) and Aneesa (born on 17 January 1994).

Boeta Oessie, like all his brothers, except Boeta Kaatjie, was a heavy smoker. He developed cancer of the lungs and died on 6 May 1988. His death left Boeta Kaatjie as the only surviving of all Saban and Gadija's children. Boeta Oessie's widow, Fatima Dreyer, survived him for 17 years, never remarrying, and died on 6 January 2005. His children and grandchildren have started a wonderful "tradition" of their own. All of them, or as many as can, get together once a month to share a meal together. Everyone brings something to eat, so no one person has to bear the burden of the catering. On one of my visits to Cape Town I was invited to attend one of these gatherings, where three generations sat down comfortably to eat and share the events of the last month.

THE EARLIEST SALASA CONNECTIONS

Abas and his sister, Sarina, are so far the earliest members of the Salasa family that I have been able to positively place in the family tree, verified by the historical records. However, in my searches I have come across others bearing the name, who I have been unable as yet to connect unequivocally with the family as we know it. Abas's parents were given as Jacob and Jeanetta Salassa, but apart from this, I have been unable to find any other trace of them in the historical records so far. They must have been alive in the 1830s because their daughter, Sarina, was born in 1835. If she was their eldest child (the evidence suggests that she was older than her brother, Abas) then one can assume that they would have been in their twenties or thirties when they married, which places their birth dates around the 1800s.

My search of the *Opgaafrolle* and *Vendu Rolls* do not reveal any Salasas, so it is possible that Jacob and Jeanetta themselves were not slaves or freed slaves. This does not mean that their parents may not have been.

The earliest record of the name Salasa is in an inventory[48] of one Maria Susanna Swart, dated 29 January 1778, of the farm Avontuur at the Brakke River. The inventory includes a slave, Salase van Ternate. Salasa may have been misspelt, Salase. This slave was not born in the Cape but came from the island of Ternaten in the Dutch East Indies. I have been unable to find out when or how Salase of Ternaten came into the possession of Maria Susanna Swart or what happened to him subsequently.

The next mention of the name is in a memorial from Achmat, Prince of Ternaten, in 1788. He had been banished to the Cape for

---

[48] KAB 8/17.3a Tanap inventories. Archives of the VOC.

a number of years and, having served his sentence of banishment, was about to return to Batavia. He asks the authorities for permission to take with him his wife, Constantia of the Cape, her mother, Dina, and her grandmother, Filida, all "of the Cape", and his children by Constantia—namely Selasa, Fatima, Camies and Abdulla.[49]

The request illustrates a number of problems for historians and genealogists. Prince Achmat obviously married a local woman from the Cape during his banishment there. Slaves born of slave mothers and settler fathers, if acknowledged by their fathers and baptised into the Church, would be manumitted and take their father's name and be accepted into the settler community. The others would remain slaves and be known as *"van de Caab"* (of the Cape). Many of these manumitted slaves would subsequently be known as "Free Blacks". A number of these were Muslims, and might enter into "relationships" with other slaves. Slave marriages were not recognised by their owners or the Dutch administration, but often slave owners would be sensitive to these Muslim marriages described as "married by Mohammedan rites", and when selling slaves on, might make it a condition that the "family" not be separated. Constantia, her mother, Dina and her grandmother, Filida, were all "of the Cape", and, therefore, fall into this category.

The second problem raised by this request is that of the status of Prince Achmat's children by Constantia. Were they slaves or manumitted slaves, and who owned them? Were they considered as Free Blacks? This would affect their status in the society of the time, as Free Blacks had a higher status in the society than ordinary slaves, although not the same status as the settlers. They could exercise their trades, own property and could even buy and sell slaves themselves. As many were Muslim, they sometimes bought slaves in order to manumit them as a religious duty.

It is not clear whether Prince Achmat's request was granted. If it was granted, and the family accompanied him to Batavia, the connection to his son, Selasa, as a possible ancestor is lost. If,

---

[49] Precis of the Archives of the Cape. Leibrandt. Requesten Number 157, 25 November 1788.

however, only Prince Achmat was allowed to leave, and not the rest of his family, the question of what happened to Selasa is of importance in the search for the ancestors. Did he remain as a slave or a Free Black? If he was a slave, who was he sold to and what were his subsequent movements in the Cape? It is tantalising to assume that Salase van Ternate and Prince Achmat's son were the same person, as Prince Achmat too was from Ternate. However, Prince Achmat's son is specifically mentioned as the son of Constantia of the Cape and must, therefore, have been born in the Cape and should really be "Salase of the Cape". Further research is needed to establish a link between Salase of Ternate, Prince Achmat of Ternate and Prince Achmat's son, Salase, and to establish which of the three, if any of them, may have been the "founding father" of the Salasas of the Cape!

Another intriguing problem raised is whether, in fact, Selasa was a male or female name. We have always assumed that Salasa was our surname, but surnames are an invention. Then, as now, in many parts of the world children took their father's name as a surname, a custom that survived well into the 19th century, even in South Africa. As an example, Great-uncle Abdol Salassa's daughter, Ameena Salassa, who married Ismail Mohamad Kasu, was also known as Ameena Abdol.

We do know from the historical record that Maria Susanna's slave, Salase, was male, but the next historical document about a Salassa illustrates the difficulty. It is a will, drawn up on 17 January 1822 by the Public Notary Jacobus Petrus de Wet, for Salassa van de Kaap, wife of Willem van de Kaap.[50] It is obvious that she is female and that both she and her husband were freed slaves. He is described as "a Free Black" and she as his "concubine" married to him "in the Mohammedan way". No mention is made of their former owners or of their children, which is a pity as it would have allowed one to trace the family and their descendents more accurately. They obviously had enough possessions for them to want to ensure that they were passed on to their issue. What is

---

[50] KAB 7/1/113 103 1822. Salassa van de Kaap, wife of Willem van de Kaap. Will.

clear is that Salassa in this case was a female first name rather than a surname.

The second will, drawn up on 7 December 1843 by the Public Notary Siewert Frederick Rörich, is for Adonis van de Kaap and his wife Salassa van de Kaap.[51] As before, Salassa is a female first name rather than a surname. Adonis is the former slave of Matthijs Lötter. The handwritten document is in very poor condition and the ink is very faded, so it is difficult to decipher, and again it gives no details of the beneficiaries, but the names are all clear. It poses several questions. Is this the same lady, Salassa van de Kaap, mentioned in the previous will 11 years earlier? If so, what happened to her then husband, Willem?

It is of course possible that Salassa van de Kaap is the same lady and that she first married Willem and later married Adonis. Willem too was a Free Black and his previous owners are not mentioned, whereas Adonis's previous owner is named as Matthijs Lötter. The other possibility is that there were two ladies living around the same time, each called Salassa van de Kaap. It is also possible that the second lady was the daughter of the first. As no beneficiaries were named in either will, we may never know the relationships of the people in these two wills. We know that Salassa and Willem were married according to Muslim rites, because their will says so, but we do not know Willem's Arabic/Muslim name.

Interestingly, The Cape Town Directory for 1833[52] lists two ladies, both named Salasia, one living at 35 Dorp Street, a few doors away from the Date Palm Mosque on the corner of Dorp and Long Streets. She is listed as a "laundress". The second Salasia is listed as a "seamstress" and lived at Kraabe-steeg. It may well be that the entries were wrong and that there was only one Salasia, who ran a business at each of the two addresses. Again, the question is, was Salasia a misspelling of Salasa, and what relation were they of the other Salasas around at the time?

---

[51] KAB 7/1/258 37 1843. Salassa van de Kaap, wife of Adonis van de Kaap. Will.
[52] Regency Cape Town by C. Pama. 1975.

To put things in context, when Salassa and Adonis's will was written in 1843, Great-grandfather Abas's sister, Sarina, would have been about seven years old and living in Malmesbury with her parents, Jacob and Jeanetta Salassa, so it may be that there were several Salassas, with branches living in Cape Town and in Malmesbury.

The next document in the Cape Town Archive is again a revealing one. It is a memorial to the Governor of the Colony, Sir George Thomas Napier, from Salasa, wife of Adonis, asking the Governor to remit the sentence passed on Adonis on 21 January 1837, when he had been sentenced to be transported to New South Wales, Australia, for seven years, for receiving stolen goods.[53] The Governor had remitted the sentence in 1839 to imprisonment with hard labour on Robben Island until February 1842. After completing two years of the remitted sentence, his wife was once again petitioning the Governor to further remit his sentence and release him, as he was sick, suffering from asthma, and because he repented his misdeed.

At the time, Salasa van de Kaap and her children were living at 7 Lynder Street, Cape Town. Adonis was by trade a saddler and was 58 years old when this petition was made, which means that he was born around 1782. Salasa herself was 42 when she made this petition, which puts her birth around 1799. Adonis would have completed his sentence on 20 February 1842, unless he had been released earlier, which is not clear from the record. However, they were both in poor health, so it may well be that the will dated 7 December 1843 was in fact theirs. To finish the story, there is a death notice for an Adonis dated 1845 that does not give the usual details about his wife or children, but it's tempting to think that this was Salasa's husband.[54] He would have been 61 years old at his death, the age around which most of the Salasas died.

I am extremely grateful to my dear friend Christiaan van der Eijk from Amsterdam for translating these documents from the

---

[53] KAB CO 4011 1 1841 Memorials Received. Salasa. Remission of confinement of her husband.
[54] MOOC 6/1/35 7671 1845 Adonis. Death Notice.

old colonial Dutch, despite the difficulties of deciphering them, as they were hand written and the ink in them was badly faded, as mentioned above.

KAMMIES SALASSA

Another unexplained link in the Salasa story is that of Kammies/ Cammies Salasa. He was a *messelaar* (bricklayer) born at Tulbagh around 1819.[55] He died on 22 July 1859 in Beaufort West, where he must have been working at the time. His wife and family must have been with him in Beaufort West when he died. His death notice gives his father as Kammies Kammies, and his mother as Kaatjie Kammies. He was married according to Mohammedan rites to a Clara Past from Worcester and had five children by her named Jumea (aged 16), Patricia (aged 11), Naomi (aged 7) and Ralea (aged two months at the time of his death). His estate was worth a considerable amount of money, in excess of a £120.

His will[56] directed that Clara and her children be taken to Worcester after his death, presumably for her and the children to be near her family, and the liquidation and distribution account[57] of his estate show that an A. Robsenburg was paid £4 to do so. Unfortunately, I have been unable to view his will, which might have shed further light on his origins and those of his family.

Rather touchingly there is a death notice[58] dated 1865 that records the death of Cammies's youngest daughter, Ralea. She was four years old when she died. It states that she was born in Beaufort West, that her father was "Salasa Kammies, deceased" and her mother was "Clara Salasa, still alive". She is said to have died at her mother's house in Worcester on 5 December 1865, and she left a small amount of money in the Guardian Fund, presumably a trust looking after the finances of orphans. She must

---

[55] MOOC 6/1/87 6205 1859 Kammies Salassa. Death Notice.
[56] MOOC 7/1/245 95 1859 Camies Salassa. Will.
[57] MOOC 13/1/183 55 1859 Camies Salassa. Liquidation and Distribution Account.
[58] MMOC 1868 Ralea Salassa. Death Notice.

have had a large inheritance from her father, Cammies Salasa, to last her the four years between his death in 1859 and hers in 1865.

So it seems that Kammies Salassa is yet another "unconnected" Salassa. Having been born in Tulbagh around 1819, of a father named Kamies, places him in the time frame of Great-grandfather Abas Salassa and his sister Sarina. Could he be a cousin, born of Jacob Salassa's brother or sister? He was born at Tulbagh, about the same distance from Malmesbury as Durbanville, and as we know, there were Salassas living in the area at the time. He was a bricklayer, which was the trade of the Salassas until the latter part of the 20th century. This might have been the reason for his first moving to Worcester and then on to Beaufort West, perhaps in search of work. He was married by Muslim law and we know for certain that at least the youngest of his daughters, Ralea, was born in Beaufort West. After his death, the family moved back to Worcester, where Ralea died, but at this point the family seems to disappear from the historical records.

SALASSA SIMONSE

This lady's first name was Salassa. According to her death notice, she was the daughter of Simon and Mamie and was born around 1825 in Cape Town.[59] She first married a Moerat Gamieldien of Paarl, by whom she had two sons—Kamaldien and Samoudien. In some of the documents the surname is given as Gamieldien, but in most it is Gamaldien. After his death in 1858, she married a Fredrik Waldpot, who owned a paint shop in Paarl. It does not seem as if she had any other children. She outlived Frederik Waldpot, who left her a rich widow. In 1879, a year before her death, she made a will,[60] which is quite detailed, leaving property in Paarl and Cape Town to her two sons and their wives. It was the custom then, as now, to make a will before going on Haj. The journey from the Cape to Saudi Arabia was long and tedious in those days and took several weeks by sea. People were often away

---

[59] MOOC 6/9/178 406 1881 Salassa Simonse. Death Notice.
[60] MOOC 7/1/414 29 & 30 1879 1880 Simonse, Salassa. Will.

from home for periods of six months to a year, so it was prudent to put one's affairs in order before undertaking the journey. Salassa was only one of many to succumb on the hazardous journey, and she died on 1 June 1880 in Mecca, Saudi Arabia.

We are once again faced with a riddle. Although this lady's first name was Salassa, her father's name was Simon, hence her surname, Simonse (belonging to Simon). If she was named after either her maternal or paternal grandmother, as was the custom of the time, as already mentioned above, the grandparent would have been a Salassa, but which grandparent was it? And exactly who this Salassa was is not clear either. As far as we know, the Salassas from whom we are descended were all living in Malmesbury at the time that this lady was born in 1825. We know that two Salassas van de Kaap—one the wife of Adonis van de Kaap and the other the wife of Willem van de Kaap—were alive at this time, so was there a connection between them and Salassa Simonse?

MY MOTHER'S FAMILY

A typical street scene in the village of Umarwada, 1998.

Our mother, Fatimah Ismail, was born on 2 May 1918 in Grahamstown in the Eastern Cape, the second daughter of Mohamed Ismail and Mariam Ismail. My grandfather was born in the village of Umarwada in the district of Broach (now called Bharuch) in present-day Gujarat. The city of Bharuch is where the River Narmada enters the Arabian Sea and it is, therefore, an important port city.

The village is a small one with only about 2,000 people, all Muslim and mostly related to each other. The nearest town is a railway junction, Ankleshwar, where in recent years oil and gas have been discovered, so the area today has become greatly industrialised. When my grandfather was born, the present-day states of Gujarat and Maharashtra constituted what was known as the Bombay Presidency and was ruled by the British from New Delhi. He was, therefore, a British subject. We came full circle when I became a British citizen in 1975!

Gujarati Muslims, like their Hindu countrymen, are either engaged in agriculture or commerce. The west coast of India has had trade links with the Persian Gulf, the Red Sea and East Africa, as well as South East Asia and the Far East, since time immemorial, and with the trade links were associated the migration of peoples. The Gujarati diaspora is proof positive of those migratory links. Many believe that Gujarat was also the point of entry of Islam into the Indian subcontinent. The oldest mosque in India, at Ghogha in Gujarat, has the *mihrab* (direction of prayer) pointing towards Jerusalem and was reputedly built between 624 and 626 AD, that is two to four years after the Hijra.

Arab traders arrived in Gujarat by sea in the first century of Islam and settled in cities along the Arabian Sea coast with their families, sometimes intermarrying with the local Muslim population, so that many Muslim families claim descent from these traders. They came from all over the Arabian Peninsula, including the cities of Medina and Taif. Many settled around the city of Surat, but they also settled in other centres like Bharuch, Anklesvar, and Ahmedabad. They were known as Bohras/Vohras or Surtis. Under the Moghuls, the port of Surat became the centre of trade relations with the Persian Gulf, East Africa and also with the newly arrived Portuguese, Dutch, English and French traders from Europe. It was also the port from which all Indian pilgrims to Mecca and Medina embarked, and thus became known as the *"Bab Makkah"* ("Gateway to Mecca"). Although the majority of Gujarati Muslims are Sunni, there is a sizeable Shia population. My grandfather was a Sunni Bohra or Surti from the heartland of the Surtis. Bharuch is about 100 miles north of Surat. A feature of the Sunni Bohra used to be that they not only spoke but also wrote Gujarati, as opposed to Urdu or Arabic. Nowadays almost everyone speaks Gujarati and Urdu.

MY GRANDPARENTS

We called my grandfather "Pa" and my grandmother "Ma". Pa was a distinguished-looking man about 5ft 6in in height. He was balding, with white hair, and fair in complexion. The photo on his certificate of identity, dated 22 February 1939, when he was about 53 years old, is how I remember him before his final illnesses. He was always well dressed in a white shirt and beautifully creased trousers. In the cooler weather he sometimes wore a pullover, and when it was really cold he would wear a jacket. He always wore a grey Trilby felt hat to protect his bald patch from the hot African sun.

Pa was softly spoken and spoke English well, with a slight Indian accent, and only very occasionally ventured an Afrikaans word, although I suspect he understood the language quite well. I also suspect that he knew quite a bit of Xhosa, although I never heard him speak it. As children, Saadia and I would always speak to him in English, which was quite a feat for us coming from Cape Town, where we mostly spoke Afrikaans to all the family.

Mum outside 8 Beaufort Street, Grahamstown, circa 1993.

Pa was a highly respected businessman in the city of Grahamstown and operated his business from a small and modest general dealer's shop at 8 Beaufort Street. At the time I first came to know it, Beaufort Street was the main road from Port Elizabeth to East London, and the shop was about halfway through the town, before one came to "the location", the shanty town where the Africans lived, now called Fingo Village. This was the ideal situation for a business of this kind, as the Africans all passed the shop on their way home after a day's work in the White areas of the town, picking up last-minute necessities, like bread, milk, coffee, etc.

Pa was respected not only by the White merchants and his White customers, but also by the local Indian community, mostly Gujaratis and most of them also business people. Although a Muslim, the local Hindus trusted him and he had quite a reputation as a mediator in disputes and as someone who could be trusted to fix business deals, something which is remembered to this day some 50 years since his death. Because he not only spoke English but also wrote it, he acted as go-between in many disputes. The local Gujarati families sent their children to him in the afternoons after "normal school" for him to teach the children to read and write Gujarati. I so regret that we were never included in the classes! He subscribed to the *Indian Opinion*, a Gujarati newspaper still published in Durban, from which he would keep abreast of the community news on a Sunday afternoon after lunch. If Saadia and I became too bored or restless, he would sit us down with a page from the paper for us "to read"!

Oral family history related by my mother has it that Pa came to South Africa at the age of around 16 with his uncle, Jeeva Essa, at the turn of the 19th century. He joined his uncle's business in Stanger for a while, but then set up on his own in the Eastern Cape, first in East London around 1902 and then in Queenstown. There are some papers missing from his immigration file in the Cape Town Archive but they confirm that Pa arrived in East London in 1902 in the then British colony of the Cape. It may be that he arrived in East London by ship from Natal, which was also a British colony but whose administration was separate from that of the Cape. The Anglo–Boer War had just ended, with the signing of the Treaty of Vereeniging in 1902. There had always been rigid restrictions on the movement of Indians between British India and the two British colonies in South Africa, as well as between the colonies and the Republic of the Transvaal and the Orange River Republic, in the days before the Union of South Africa was formed in 1910.

It was here that he met and married Ma, on 13 November 1907 in the Independent Church in Queenstown.[61] He was aged 24 and she was 23. They had their first child, Ismail, here the following year. They moved to Grahamstown in 1910 and lived there until the end of their lives.

Ma was born Maria Johanna Le Roux and became Mariam Ismail on her marriage to Pa. She was about the same height as Pa, fair in complexion, and at the time I knew her, she already had long, grey hair, always tidy and covered with a scarf. She was quite stout in build and

Mariam Ismail, born Maria Johanna Le Roux.

---

[61] Marriage Certificate among her estate papers.

Mariam Ismail (Ma) in a
shalwaar qameez.

always wore long skirts that reached below her calves. For special occasions she would wear a *shalwar qameez* with a long scarf. Her only ornaments were her wedding ring and four gold bangles on each arm. When she died, Mum and Auntie each inherited four of these bangles. When Mum died, each of her four children received one of Mum's four. I wear mine in remembrance of Ma.

Ma had an air of authority about her and ruled her children and the household servants with a rod of iron. She was equally strict with her sisters and brothers, and although she was not the eldest in her family, they respected her opinions and judgement. Behind the strict facade she was the kindest of people. She always had people staying at short notice who had to be fed and needed somewhere to bed down. The African people from the Transkei named her after their goddess of charity. They always had somewhere to stay when they came to sell their animals and produce in the markets in Grahamstown. They would bring her gifts of rare species of fowl they had trapped near their homes in the Transkei and repaid her generosity by cleaning, housework and gardening. She was house-proud to the point of obsession. She spoke fluent Xhosa and always spoke to Saadia and me in Afrikaans. We spoke the Cape dialect of Afrikaans but always lost it within days of arriving in Grahamstown for the "purer" Afrikaans spoken by the Afrikaner.

Ma loved farming and animals, I suppose due to her ancestry. In the backyard of the house in Chapel Street, which is my earliest memory of Grahamstown, she had various breeds of chickens, ducks, geese and dogs. The latter were really watchdogs, and they really frightened Saadia and me, let alone any prospective burglars! She also had a herd of cattle on some land that she owned in Riebeeck East, and sheep and goats on land in the Transkei.

Whenever we visited Grahamstown, a cow would be brought from the herd and tethered on a patch of grass at the bottom of William Street so that we could have fresh milk, even though they sold milk in the shop! Because there were no Halal butchers in Grahamstown, Pa would slaughter chickens in order for us to have fresh meat, at a time when chicken was considered a great delicacy and very expensive. Otherwise, we ate

Ma with Bahia, wife of Sheikh Ismail Moos, circa 1950.

Gujarati vegetarian curries. When we had visitors from neighbouring towns or the Moos family from Cape Town, Pa would slaughter a sheep or a goat in honour of the visitors.

Ma also loved growing things. She was a member of the Bathurst Farmers' Union and read the *Farmer's Weekly*, their official publication, for pleasure! She had a large "kitchen garden" in Chapel Street and an orchard at 6 Beaufort Street, next to the shop, when they moved there from Chapel Street in the late 1940s. She had apple, plum, lemon and peach trees and even a vine, although it bore only very small and very sour berries! All this in spite of the fact that they sold all these fruits in the shop next door!

ISMAIL MOHAMED ISMAIL (MOOLLA)

Apart from Ismail, their eldest son, they had five more children— Ahmed, Hawa (or "Gall" as she was known), Sulaiman (or "Sol"), Fatimah (my mother) and Ebrahim (or "Ebie"). The eldest son, Ismail Mohamed, born in Queenstown on 20 November 1908, died on 22 February 1936 at the age of 28. I have as yet been unable to obtain his death certificate, so I don't know exactly what he died of. Mum used to say that both her older brothers died of pneumonia or tuberculosis. Ismail's grave in the family plot in the Albany Road Cemetery in Grahamstown had a marble headstone engraved in Arabic reading, "This is the sad grave of Ismail, the son of Mohamed

Ismail", followed in English by the date of his death. When I had the graves restored in 2004, I specified that the old headstone be retained.

AHMED ISMAIL (MOOLLA)

Ahmed Ismail (Moolla).

Ahmed Ismail was born in 1911 in Burghersdorp—where, incidentally, Ma was also born—and died on 11 October 1930, at the age of 19, in Grahamstown. It may well be that Ma was on a visit to her parents at Burghersdorp when he was born, as this was a year after the family had moved to Grahamstown. Family legend has it that both brothers had been sent to the boarding school at Miah's farm in the Transvaal, and the terrible conditions in the boarding school had so weakened them that they were subject to chest infections, which eventually caused their premature death. In any event, the death of the two brothers left Ma emotionally scarred for the rest of her life. She never again slept in a bed, insisting on sleeping on a mattress on the floor, because her two sons were "sleeping under the earth". We would all go the Albany Road Cemetery, where their graves were, on Sunday afternoons. Ma would weep at the graves as if they had died the day before.

Pa and Ma were devoted to each other and would not hear a bad word said about each other. They were married just 49 years when Ma died in 1956. Pa died almost a year to the day later.

HAWA COOPER, born ISMAIL (MOOLLA)

Saadia and I called our only maternal aunt, Hawa (Gall) "Galatie". I've explained the derivation of this word above, but it meant that we had two Galaties—Bie's sister and Mum's sister! After Rush was born, we got into the habit of calling her "Auntie", like Rush did. Auntie was about 5ft 8in, fair, with long, shiny black hair that reached down to her waist. She wore her hair in a plait when working in the shop or the house but in a bun on social occasions, like most Gujarati women. She was a very beautiful woman but had a fierce temper. She too was extremely house-proud and spent all her waking hours scrubbing, cleaning, washing and ironing. She eloped to marry Govinda Cupusamy, or

Hawa Cooper (Gall), born Ismail Moolla, 8 Scott Street, South End, Port Elizabeth, 1957.

Frank Cooper as he preferred to be known, a Tamil waiter from Port Elizabeth, and they settled down in a small terraced house in Scott Street, South End, obliquely opposite the Pier Street Mosque. He worked as a waiter and barman in the golf club at Humewood and later as a furniture salesman. He must have been better dressed than his bosses, as Auntie made sure that he was always well turned out. By

contrast, she neglected herself, wore no make-up and spent not a penny on a wardrobe for herself. She devoted herself and all her resources to him and looked like his housekeeper rather than his wife. They had no children. When Rush was born shortly after Boeja Joe had had his first heart attack, Auntie wanted to adopt her to help ease the financial burden on my parents, but they could not bear the thought of splitting up the family, so the plan was abandoned.

Frank Cooper, Donkin Memorial, Port Elizabeth, 1957.

Frank was a philanderer, although charming. He was dark in complexion like most Tamils and his hair was always slicked back with Brilliantine. As I mentioned, he was always elegantly dressed in a suit with matching tie. Auntie herself even polished his shoes daily. He spoke little

**Frank and Fatima Dreyer,
Boeta Osman's wife.**

Afrikaans but very good English, useful in his work as a waiter and salesman. He visited Cape Town on holiday twice as far as I can recall, and there are some photos of him with Karriem Salasa and also Sis Fatima, Boeta Oessie's wife. Auntie never came on holiday with him, always insisting that she could not leave the house locked up and unattended. She considered even her trips to Grahamstown as "a duty" to look after the family graves rather than as a holiday, and similarly when she came to Cape Town to visit us.

It was only months before Auntie died on 29 May 1984 that it became known that Frank had had a mistress for some years and had had several children by her. After Auntie died, she and the children moved in with him into the house in Malabar, the Indian area of Port Elizabeth, which they had been forced to move to under the Group Areas Act. They lived there together until he died on 13 May 1985, less than a year after Auntie.

Auntie is buried in the Muslim cemetery in Malabar, Port Elizabeth.

SULAIMAN ISMAIL (MOOLLA)

**Sulaiman Ismail (Moolla)
Uncle Sol.**

My Uncle Sol/Sulaiman was a bit of a black sheep in the family. He had always been mischievous, even as a child. Mum used to relate how he would spend his pocket money getting stray donkeys out of the local pound! In one incident while playing with a catapult, he was shot in the eye and it could not be saved, so he was blind in that eye to the end of his life. It is quite evident in the one passport-sized photo I have of him. He was tall and fair and I always remember him wearing khaki shirt and shorts during the holidays, as was the wont of the Afrikaners.

He seemed to spend long periods estranged from Ma and Pa because of what they considered as his "wayward behaviour", and when we visited from Cape Town, we were never allowed to meet him and his wife. However, Mum always managed to surreptitiously meet with him, and on these occasions *we* did too.

He had married the divorced wife of a Chinese merchant from East London. She was an Afrikaner called Kate. She disliked the Ismails and anyone associated with them, but she softened when it came to us children. She never understood that we were not allowed to play with her son, Eddie, by her earlier marriage. She and Uncle Sol never had children of their own, but he accepted and reared Eddie as his own. Kate was several years older than Uncle Sol and predeceased him by several years. By this time, he had spent his not inconsiderable inheritance from his parents, something they had always feared would happen, and he was in poor health because of hypertension and heart disease. He spent the rest of his life living in a mobile home, travelling between Grahamstown, East London and Port Alfred, where he always spent every summer fishing. A few months before his death, Auntie invited him to live with her and Frank in Malabar. He parked his mobile home in her backyard so he could be "independent" and she could be sure that he had a decent meal. However, it was not a happy situation, as he and Frank had never got on and Auntie would always side with Frank in any argument. He died a week before her, in May 1984, and is buried in the Muslim cemetery in Malabar, Port Elizabeth.

Ebrahim Ismail (Moolla)
Uncle Ebie

EBRAHIM ISMAIL (MOOLLA)

Mum's youngest brother was called Ebrahim/Ebie. He was born in Grahamstown around 1922. As the youngest of the children, he was somewhat spoilt. He was the apple of Ma's eye and was to be one of the causes of great distress to her at the end of her life. He was tall like my mother and fair like all his brothers and sisters. It is said that he spoke Xhosa so well that many of the Xhosa elders marvelled at his command of the language.

When he reached his early twenties, Pa persuaded Ma that it was time he was married, an idea which she was not keen on. She had lost her two eldest sons, Uncle Sol had made an "unsatisfactory" marriage and she was anxious for her youngest son.

Apparently, Pa had wanted to arrange a marriage for Ahmed, the second eldest, as was the custom among the Indian community, but Ma was against the idea and rejected all the proposed girls. When he died, she blamed herself for having been too proud to accept any of the girls proposed for him on the grounds that they were not good enough for him, guilt that stayed with her till the end of her life. When it came to Ebie's marriage, she relented, not wanting a repeat of what had happened to Ahmed.

A marriage was, therefore, arranged to a girl from a neighbouring town whose parents came from the same area of Gujarat that Pa had come from. Hanifa Haffejee was similar in age to Uncle Ebie and as tall and fair as he was. She was a "traditional" Indian girl who wore a *shalwar qameez* and stayed at home and cooked and cleaned the home, although there were always servants to do the menial jobs. The couple lived at 11 Chapel Street, next to number 12 where Pa and Ma lived. An "outing" for her would be to go to the family shop in Beaufort Street and spend an afternoon "helping out", as there were no other Indian Muslim girls of her age to visit or to be friends with. Her two sisters-in-law were married, Auntie living in Port Elizabeth and Mum in Cape Town. But to her this was no different to what she had been used to with her family in her own town. Unfortunately, the marriage did not last and after a while they divorced and she returned to her parents. Hanifa subsequently remarried and I have heard that she found happiness in her new marriage. She and Uncle Ebie had no children. In retrospect, I think Uncle Ebie had problems with relationships and this was the reason that the marriage failed.

Uncle Ebie died in the middle of October 1954, about a month after Rush was born. He had had a heart attack during the night and died in his sleep. Ma went to wake him in the morning as she usually did, with a cup of coffee, it being his turn to go the market to buy the fresh produce for the shop, and found him dead. She never recovered from the shock. He was only 33 years old. Ma herself died of carcinoma of the gall bladder little more than a year after him on 1 February 1956[62] at the age of 72, and they are buried side by side in the family plot.

Fatimah Salasa, born Ismail, before her marriage to Bie, circa 1941.

FATIMAH ISMAIL (MOOLLA)

My mother, Fatimah, was the youngest but one of my grandparents' children and the younger of their two daughters. She was born in Grahamstown on 2 May 1918. She was named after her paternal

aunt, Fatimah, Pa's eldest sister. As a child, Mum had the reputation of being a bit of a tomboy. She rode a bicycle and climbed trees like her brothers and she broke both her humeri and a leg as a child! She was rather spoilt as the younger of the two girls. As a young woman, she was tall by the standards of the day, at 5ft 10in, and slim and very fair. Like Auntie, she had very long, shiny, black hair; Indian girls at the time were not allowed to cut their hair,

Fatima Salasa, born Ismail, after her marriage to Bie, circa 1943.

[62] MOOC 6/9/23951 1563/56 Ismail, Mariam, nee Le Roux. Estate Papers. 1956.

but she wore it in an elegant bun with the front waved over her forehead, as was the fashion of the time. I have a photo of her about a year before she married Bie showing how elegant she was. She only cut her hair for the first time in the early 1970s, after Bie had died, and from then on wore it very short.

I don't think Pa and Ma approved of Mum marrying Bie, although this was never spoken of in the family. I suspect that it was because he was not Indian and also the fear that his job as a bricklayer might not provide sufficient income for them to live on. Although there is no "caste system" among the Muslim communities of Gujarat as there is among the Hindus, Muslim marriages are contracted between people of similar social and financial standing. As Mum came from a well-off trading family and Bie came from a less well-off labouring family, such a marriage would traditionally have been considered "unequal" and, therefore, unacceptable. However, it did not take them long to accept him, as at least he was Muslim, albeit of the Shafi'i school of Islamic jurisprudence, while Pa, like the majority of Indians, followed the Hanafi school! I know for certain that Bie was more readily accepted than Uncle Frank, who was not even welcome to stay with them at either Chapel Street or at 6 Beaufort Street, where they eventually moved to, whereas Bie stayed with them at both houses whenever he visited them in Grahamstown. Like all marriages, that of my parents' had its ups and downs, but they made it work in their own way. They had been married about 31 years when Bie died unexpectedly of a heart attack on 3 August 1973. Mum never remarried and remained a widow for the 29 years until her own death on 30 August 2002.

I was the eldest of their four children and the only son. I was born on 3 December 1942 at 28 Goldsmith Road, where my parents were living with my paternal grandparents, Boeja/Saban and Ummie/Gadija. They moved shortly after I was born to 24 Goldsmith Road, where they shared the house with Bie's "second cousin" Achmat Brown and his wife Safia (see above under "The Brown Connection"). Saban sold numbers 24 and 26 Goldsmith Road in 1945, so we moved to 59 Fenton Road with Achmat and Fiah Brown, who a few months later moved to Constantia to a larger and very beautiful house.

SAADIA VALLEY-OMAR, born SALASA

Saadia is about two and a half years younger than me and was born at 59 Fenton Road. I think everyone expected that with a child of each sex our family would be complete, but these were the days before birth control and some seven years later Rush was born! Saadia was always a rather delicate child, who later in her teens developed asthma. She was very fair in complexion and had beautiful long hair, which Mum or I plaited daily. There was a fair amount of sibling rivalry between us, being so close in age. Whereas I went to Habibia in Thornhill, which in those days was a long way from Salt River—involving a train journey to Mowbray and then an even longer bus journey to the

Rush and Saadia. 28 Goldsmith Road, Salt River. 2007.

Rayanah, Sonny, Saadia, Fatima, Shamiema and Rushdeyah. May 2010.

school, and back again in the afternoon—Saadia was thought to be too delicate to travel that far to school, so she went to Salt River Primary School, two streets away. When it came to a primary school having to be chosen for me, there were endless debates as to whether it ought to be a "Muslim" school (there was one in Kipling Street, Salt River, which Bie had attended and which was used by the local Malay community)

Shamiema, Zubayr and Fatima. April, 2010.

or one of the "secular" schools nearby. The choice of Habibia (a school for the children of the local Indian community) for my primary education was, I think, a concession to Mum and her parents.

Both Saadia and I went to Trafalgar High School to do our Junior and Senior Certificates—not quite overlapping, but taught by more or less the same set of teachers. I think she arrived at Trafalgar the year after I left, which was of no help to her, as all the teachers knew me and comparisons were frequently made to her disadvantage!

Saadia then went on to do nursing at Groote Schuur Hospital, rotating through some of the other teaching hospitals in Cape Town. Despite obtaining nursing qualifications in Psychiatry, Obstetrics and Paediatrics, she opted to work in Geriatrics until her retirement in 2009.

She married Mohamed Valley-Omar (Bhai) in 1968. He was then a medical student. Bhai and I had been at Trafalgar High School together in the late 1950s, and quite coincidentally were born on the same day of the same month in the same year (3 December 1942). Even more strange was the fact that we both had the same blood group, one of the rarest—AB rhesus negative! Bhai came from a prominent family of business people in Worcester. His grandparents too were from Gujarat, although he seemed to express little interest in his family's past at the time.

Rushdeyah Gamieldien, formerly Samsodien, born Salasa, with Sonny, April 2008.

Saadia and Bhai have three surviving children—Rayanah, Shamiema and Fatima. Saadia had a few miscarriages and at least one stillborn son before the girls were born.

When they were first married, and as both of them were still studying—he at the University of Cape Town and she at Groote Schuur Hospital— they lived at 28 Goldsmith

Road, and it was here that Rayanah was born on 21 July 1973, just a few weeks before Bie died.

As soon as Bhai qualified, he and Saadia moved to Worcester to live with his parents, but this caused some friction and they moved to Beaufort West, where Bhai set up as a general practitioner. By this time, Shamiema and Fatima were babes in arms. Unfortunately, the marriage started to deteriorate and they finally divorced. Bhai remarried twice after the divorce but there were no further children from those marriages as far as I know. Saadia never remarried.

RUSHDEYAH GAMIELDIEN, formerly SAMSODIEN, born SALASA

Rushdeyah was born on Friday, 13 August 1954. Mum and Bie had told Saadia and me about the impending birth and we were very much involved in all the preparations for the new arrival. I even knitted little booties for the new baby! Rush is shorter in stature than Saadia, Fow or me, and darker in complexion than we are. As I was about 12 when she was born, I was actively involved in caring for her during the early years. I bathed the baby, changed her nappies, fed her, and when the time came, took her to school. She remembers going to the same primary school as Saadia and remembers her first "traumatic" day at school when I left her with her new teacher! Apparently, I told her I was going to the toilet and only reappeared to take her home when school finished for the day!

Rush has always been sensitive and easily hurt. She was utterly devoted to both our parents. Bie's death greatly scarred her. To this day, 37 years later, she tends to his grave, has a recital of the Qur'an on the anniversary of his death and puts flowers on his grave on the anniversary of his birth. She was 18 years old when he died and was at Wesley Teacher Training College, completing her teaching qualification. With me abroad in exile and Saadia married with three small children, Rush felt responsible for the young Fow, who was about 11 years old at the time of Bie's death. She felt pressured to finish college in order to get a job to support Mum, not knowing that I was already doing so.

I also think that this bereavement influenced her personal relationships. She married Abe (Abduragiem) Samsodien on 26 September 1981. For reasons I do not know, the marriage was not a success and they were divorced on 11 August 1986. They had had no children, so she returned home to 28 Goldsmith Road, where she and Mum formed a very close, mutually dependent relationship that seemed to exclude her marrying again and that lasted until the end of Mum's life. About a year after Mum's death in 2002, Rush rather suddenly and unexpectedly married an old family friend, Dr Abdullah Gamieldien. Within weeks she discovered he was psychologically unwell and the marriage was annulled. They remained friends and she continued to be supportive to him when he had a stroke. Sadly, he died in 2008.

FOWZIYAH ABRAHAMS, born SALASA

Setting out for Fowziyah's graduation April 2010.

I was 19 and in my first year at university when Fow was born on 6 September 1961. Unlike when Rush was born, none of us even realised Mum was pregnant with Fow! I arrived home from university one afternoon to find Mum in bed with the new baby! Saadia was about 17 and about to finish high school and Rush was about seven and still at primary school. Bie must have been about 45 and Mum 43 years old, so they were "elderly parents", with effectively two "families", namely, Saadia and me, and Rush and Fow! Again it fell on me to help out caring for the two children, as Saadia was severely asthmatic and Bie was not terribly domesticated. As a result, Rush and Fow have always regarded me as a "substitute parent", something that became more poignant when Bie died 11 years later.

Mum, who had always been very strict when Saadia, Rush and I were growing up, seemed more relaxed about allowing me to change her normal "child-raising routine" with Fow. I think it may have been due to the fact that I was a medical student and within reach of becoming a doctor. Most people of their generation had great respect for doctors, so whenever I suggested to Mum that we should allow Fow to do certain things or allow her a laxity in expressing herself in a

Standing: Ayesha, Rashied (Adnaan's parents) and two of his sisters, March 1986.

way that for the time seemed "too open", she acquiesced so that Fow, and to a lesser extent Rush, grew up in a more "liberal" way than Saadia or me. Fow became very attached to me and I think it was a great wrench for her when I went into exile in April 1968, when she was around six or seven years old. It must have been like being "abandoned" by a parent, although she has never said so or complained. At the time it seemed that I would never see them again, so it was as traumatic for me as it was for them.

Bie's death affected us all in different ways and left psychological scars that I suspect we bear to this day. Mum somehow managed to keep things together for the two younger ones, and Fow grew up into a spirited and confident young woman. People remark on the physical resemblance between us. She is tall and fair with grey eyes. After completing teacher training, she followed Rush into teaching, specialising in mathematics.

She married Adnaan Abrahams on 29 March 1986. Adnaan is the only son of Rashied and Ayesha Abrahams, who at the time lived a few doors away from us in Goldsmith Road. He is a week younger than Fow, so we often joke that they knew each other "in the womb" when our mothers would meet!

His father worked with Bie on several jobs, most notably on the campus of Stellenbosch University, at that time the premier Afrikaans university in the country, and one of the bastions of White supremacy. Several years later, when the university decided

Fowziyah Abrahams, born Salasa, graduation ceremony, April 2010.

Zubayr and Maryam, 16 St Saviours Court, December 2007.

to admit non-White students, Adnaan was one of the first to graduate from there.

Adnaan's degree was in forestry, which meant that he needed to enter government service and move to wherever he was posted. After their marriage, his first posting was in Knysna, after which they moved several times. One of his most memorable jobs was as curator of Kirstenbosch, the botanical gardens known as "the Kew of the Southern Hemisphere". He was the first non-White to hold the position. Fow followed me to study education as a mature student at the University of Cape Town, my alma mater. Halfway through the degree, she had to transfer to Rhodes University in Grahamstown to complete the degree, as Adnaan was working in East London at the time and the whole family had had to move there. She graduated with a B.Ed (Hons) from Rhodes in April 2009, and I was privileged and proud to be present at the ceremony. It is ironic that she graduated in Grahamstown, where Mum was born, from the university to which her maternal grandfather supplied fruit, vegetables and other commodities more than half a century previously.

Fow and Adnaan have three children—Zubayr (born on 26 May 1988), Maryam (born on 15 May 1990) and Nabil (born on 25 June 1995). Zubayr followed me to study at the University of Cape Town, while Maryam followed her father and enrolled to do Medical Sciences at the University of Stellenbosch. She had to abandon her studies when the family moved to Western Australia in January 2010. She is hoping to enrol at either Perth or Sydney to study Physiotherapy or Medicine in September 2010.

THE ISMAILS (MOOLLA)

As mentioned above, oral family history has it that Pa came to South Africa from Gujarat with an uncle, Jeewa Essa, around 1899 when he was aged about 16. They were in business in Stanger, but Pa decided to leave Natal and settle in the Eastern Cape. I have as yet been unable to find the historical record to verify this bit of the story, but there is mention in his immigration papers of a "Domicile Certificate",[63] presumably a form of residency permit, dated 1899, stating that he is in business in Verulam, Natal. Verulam is not far from Stanger, so this is not implausible but needs further investigation.

What I have been able to establish positively, is that Pa came to East London by sea and landed there in 1902. At the time, Indians were subject to several immigration controls which required them to give details about their physical characteristics, country of origin, parents and siblings, place of residence and all their movements after entry into the country. This was a requirement for the two British colonies (Natal and the Cape Colony) and also the two Boer Republics (the Transvaal Republic and the Orange River Republic). After the formation of the Union of South Africa in 1910, the new Department of the Interior of the Union had a special Department of Immigration and Asiatic Affairs to control the movement of Indians between the four provinces of the Union. Control of the movement of Indians continued until the fall of the racists in 1994, and I recall that even in my lifetime, Indians had to have a permit even just to transit the Orange Free State if it was going to take them longer than 24 hours. As these regulations did not apply to Coloureds or Malays, it sometimes suited Indians to pretend they were Malay. Although the restrictions were onerous and a clear violation of human

---

[63] Domicile Certificate No 5092. 18 November 1899. Business at Verulam.

rights, causing untold suffering and misery, the records and documentation do help present-day researchers to plot the movement of individuals and families. And so it was with Pa.

Although there are several documents missing from Pa's immigration file in the Cape Town Archives, there is enough to piece together his movements with a degree of certainty.[64] The earliest document in his file is dated 1933, when he applied to visit Natal with his son Ahmed. It confirms that he did in fact first enter the Cape Colony in 1902 and that he stayed in East London for two years until 1904. There had been an outbreak of the Plague in East London in 1902, for which Asian immigrants were blamed. A restriction of the movement of people out of the city was meant to contain the spread of the disease, and must have done so, for Pa was able to move to Queenstown in 1904, where he stayed until 1909, before moving on to Grahamstown in 1910. He is by trade a general dealer and at the time (1933) was living at 12 Chapel Street in Grahamstown. Everything in the file confirms oral family history, that his wife was Maria Johanna Le Roux and names all their children and their ages. It is interesting that his height is recorded as being 5ft 4in, whereas later it is given as 5ft 8in, and he is recorded as having a scar on the shin of his right leg, which I can personally confirm.

Pa aged about 52 years old, Circa 1938

PA'S PARENTS

Pa's parents were Ismail Barber and Amaboo Ismail. By 1934 his father had died, but his mother was still alive and living in the village of Umarwada, in the then British Presidency of Bombay. The State of Gujarat only came into existence in 1961.

---

[64] IRC 1/1/908 12830A 1934 Immigration Papers Mahomed Ismail and his daughters Fatima and Hawa.

The same convention about the naming of children discussed above in relation to the Meyers and Salasas are applicable to Muslim South Asian families; thus, Pa's name was Mahomed, the son of Ismail (Barber), hence Mahomed Ismail. A *moolla* is a Muslim priest, so it is likely that Pa's grandfather was a priest or imam and his family would be known as Moolla or "from the family of the Moolla", which later became their surname.

Pa's mother, Amaboo, was born Amaboo Kasim Moolla and took her husband's name on her marriage to Barber Ismail, becoming Amaboo Ismail. She was born at Umarwada around 1868. Her father would have been Kasim Moolla, hence her "maiden name" Kasim Moolla. When Barber Ismail, her husband, died (date uncertain), she married a widower, Mahomed Ebrahim Kazee, and became Amaboo Kazee.[65]

Pa's stepfather, Mahomed Ebrahim Kazee, is reported to have accepted him as his "son". His daughter, Pa's stepsister, Bai Hawa, married a cousin, Bawa Gulam Kazee, from the neighbouring village of Ankrod, about six or seven miles away from Umarwada. They were a religious family and very involved in the religious politics of the time. In fact, their grandson is a *molvi* (an expert/teacher of Islamic law) by the name of Ayub Kazee and now lives in Umarwada. Pa's stepfather, the latter's sons-in-law and brothers were all involved in furthering the cause of the Barelvi movement of the 1870/80s. They are known as the *Ahle Sunnat Wal Jamaat* (People of the Traditions of Muhammad and the Broad Community) and base their beliefs on the Qur'an and the *Sunnah* (practices) of the Prophet. They follow the Ash'ari and Maturdi School of *aqida* (creed or belief systems), the Hanafi School of *fiqh* (Islamic jurisprudence) and they tend to embrace the Qadri, Chisthi, Naqshbandi or Suhrawardi Sufi orders.

The Barelvi movement, although quite "liberal" in outlook, was part of a movement started in Bareilly, in Uttar Pradesh, India, to revive the "true values of Islam" in India. They were, therefore, a kind of "revivalist" movement at the time, and as

---

[65] Kazee or Kajee. A *qadi* is an Islamic judge.

such were opposed to the Indian Congress Party led by Gandhi and Nehru in the struggle for Indian independence from British rule, suspicious that the latter wanted to establish a Hindu state in which the Muslims would be deprived of their civic rights and the freedom to practise their religion. They, therefore, condemned the Muslims in the Congress Party as "traitors to the Muslim cause". They were also opposed to the use of force in resistance to British rule, as they considered the British to be "People of the Book" and, therefore, although "misguided", not to be deposed by force. It is history that the Congress Party won the battle for political power in the newly independent India. Although Muslims have had difficult times in India since independence over 60 years ago, India remains nominally a secular state, where everyone can practise their religion freely.

The successors of the Barelvi movement today are spread all over India, Pakistan and Afghanistan, and they are today a "moderate" force in Islamic politics. Commendably, they oppose the wilful destruction of all human life by the Jihadis and the "Talibanisation" of Afghanistan and Pakistan, and they have been targeted by these organisations for their beliefs. Their mosques and *madrassas* (religious schools) have been bombed, resulting in great loss of life.

When Mohamed Ebrahim Kazee, her second husband, died, Amaboo did not marry again. Pa applied to the Department of Immigration and Asiatic Affairs in 1940, after his return from his only visit to India in 1939 (see below), for her to be allowed to visit him in Grahamstown to introduce her to his family. She was about 72 years old at the time and in poor health, but the application was refused. She died the following year and is buried in her native village of Umarwada.

Pa applied to visit Durban in 1937 by car, specifically not passing through the Transkei, and the permit was issued, dated 24 November 1937. As this was the beginning of the summer holiday season, it may well have been the visit when Ma accompanied him, rather than the visit of 1933/4. Being South African born, Ma would not have needed a permit to travel anywhere within the South African borders. Mum would have been about 19 at the time. Auntie was married and aged 23 and Uncle Sol about 21, so they would have been old enough to be left on their own and well able to look after the business while their parents were away on holiday. It may have been on this visit that the famous gold bangles made from melted gold sovereigns were made for Ma by an Indian jeweller in Durban.

Pa returned to India for a visit on 26 March 1939, the first time he had returned to his homeland since 1902 (or perhaps 1899). He had been resident in South Africa for 37 years and had not seen his mother or sisters in all that time. The local Grahamstown newspaper[66] reported the event in their "Personalia" column:

"Mr Mahomed Ismail left by last night's train for Durban en-route to India, where he will spend a short holiday with his mother after an absence of 37 years."

By all accounts this visit was traumatic for the family, as war was looming. Pa had been granted a Certificate of Identity (a form of passport for Indians)[67] stating that he had to return to South Africa by February 1942 or lose his right of residency, and although his holiday was planned to be for about six months, if war did break out, he may not have been able to return before the Certificate of Identity expired. As it happened, the Second World War did break out in September 1939. Oral history has it that Pa hastened to return to South Africa. His ship, the SS *Kenya*, was torpedoed by a German submarine off the East African coast (Tanganyika, present-day Tanzania, was then a German colony) but they were not badly damaged and managed to reach Durban on 15 November 1939,[68] where they were promptly quarantined on Salisbury Island by the Union Government!

Communications were poor and the family in Grahamstown had not had any news of him for many weeks and presumed that he had either been killed or was not returning home until the end of the war. However, the quarantine was lifted and he was allowed

---

[66] *Grocott's Daily Mail*, Tuesday, 21 March, 1939.
[67] Certificate of Identity No 12351, dated 22 February 1939.
[68] SS *Kenya*, Deck Passenger, List 8.

to return to the Cape Province on 20 November 1939.[69] One can but imagine the scene when he unexpectedly walked into the house on 23 November 1939! The local newspaper reported the following day:

"Mr Mahomed Ismail arrived in the city by car yesterday from Durban after eight months' holiday in India."[70]

PA AS A BUSINESSMAN

Bearing in mind that Pa and Ma moved to Grahamstown in 1910 with two children, aged one and three years old, they must have worked hard to start a successful business. The 1916 Voters' Roll, six years after their arrival in the city, shows them as the owner-occupiers of a house in William Street. The number of the house is not shown, but then, as now, William Street was only a small street with about a dozen houses, six on each side of the road. I suspect that it was either number 6, 7 or 10, as all of these properties remained in the family until the 1950s. It was in number 10 William Street that Auntie (Hawa) was born in October 1913, so the evidence is strong that this is the house mentioned in the 1916 Voters' Roll.

Pa was becoming established as a businessman in Grahamstown. The family moved from the smaller house in William Street to the White business area of town. The 1921 "Port Elizabeth and Midlands Directory" lists Pa as "Mahomet Ismail, Forwarding Agent" living at 10 Chapel Street. He presumably still owned 10 William Street. The 1934 Voters' Roll has him down for two properties—10 Chapel Street and 35 Beaufort Street—both in the White area of town, which meant that he had two votes in the municipal elections, which was based on ownership of immovable property. Number 35 Beaufort Street still exists. It is now a listed building in the White area of town, opposite Rhodes University. Intriguingly, the same Voters' Roll also has a Wilhelmina Theodora Le Roux living at 11 Chapel Street. Numbers 10, 11 and 12 Chapel

---

[69] Immigration Regulation Act 1913. Permit No 12830 A.
[70] *Grocott's Daily Mail*, Friday, 24 November 1939.

Street are a row of cottages that still exist, although now heavily modernised, and Pa might have bought number 11 from Wilhelmina Theodora Le Roux. She is obviously a relation of Ma's, but I have been unable to trace the connection.

Rush, Fatima Jeewa
(Mohammed Ismail's mother),
Mum and Hajiera (his wife),
Umarwada, Gujarat, 1998.

The 1937 Voters' Roll shows the extent of the family's property holdings. Pa still owns 10 Chapel Street, and also 10 William Street. Pa and Ma had a policy of giving each of their children a property when they reached the age of 21. The property was rented out and the rent was theirs to do with as they pleased. Thus it is that Uncle Ahmed is registered as the owner of 10 Beaufort Street, a two- storey house next to the shop, although we know from other sources that Ahmed died in 1933. It may well be that after his death Pa and Ma neglected to update themselves on the Electoral Register, but the property would have reverted back to them anyway as Ahmed was unmarried and had no children.

The 1937 Voters' Roll also shows Suliaman Ismail (Uncle Sol) owning 18 Wylde Street. This was the row of cottages where Ma's father and brother, Dr Abdol, had lived before they died. Pa and Ma owned several of the cottages, and one of them was given to Mum. In the 1950s the South African Railways compulsorily purchased half the houses in Wylde Street in order to expand the railway goods yard. They "compensated" Mum with a pitifully small sum for her property around 1957. Today there are only about six houses left in Wylde Street, one of which is the house that Ma's father, David Mentor Le Roux, had lived in.

PA'S BROTHER, JEEWA ISHAQ MOOLLA

Mum's cousin, still living in Umarwada, tells me that Pa had a brother, Jeewa Ishaq Moolla, who also came to South Africa, but he was unable to give me the exact date. He settled in Stanger,

Natal, where he eventually died. His son, Ismail Mohamed Jeewa, returned to India with his wife, Fatima Ismail Jeewa, and settled in the family's home village of Umarwada. We met their two sons, Mohamed Ismail and Yacob Ismail, and their families when we visited India in 1998, and I am still in touch with them periodically. If the links are correct, then their father, Ismail Mohamed Jeewa Moolla, was Mum's first cousin, and they are our second cousins.

Pa's brother, Jeewa Ishaq Moolla, had two other sons—Dawood Ishaq Jeewa (Moolla) and Ahmed Ishaq Jeewa. Dawood Ishaq Jeewa (Moolla) lived in Stanger. His son, Ismail, is today a dentist and lives in Rondebosch, Cape Town, and when Dawood and his wife visited their son, Ismail, they all met up with Mum. Dawood is, thus, Mum's first cousin. Dawood Ishaq died tragically in a road traffic accident shortly after this meeting. I continue to have tenuous links with Ismail, and he and his wife, Ayesha, were very supportive to us when Mum died in 2002.

Ahmed Ishaq Jeewa lives in Durban, but I have no more information about him or his family. He too would be Mum's first cousin. It may well be that Pa came to South Africa with his uncle, but it may also be that Mum misheard the story and that he actually came with his brother, Jeewa Ishaq Moolla. They set up in business in Stanger but then Pa went to East London to branch out on his own.

Mohammed Ismail Jeewa and Mum, with our driver, Umarwada, Gujarat, 1998.

PA'S SISTERS

FATIMA GULAM MOOLLA MOOSAJIE

Mum always said that Pa had a sister called Fatima, after whom she was named, and a second sister Aishabai. Apparently, Mum was temperamentally more like her Aunt Aisha. In Pa's application for his mother to visit him in 1940, he declared that he had no

brothers but two sisters—
Aishabai, and Fatima, the latter
married to Gulam Moolla
Moosajie. At this time, Gulam
had been dead for about 17
years, so he had probably died
around 1923. Fatima herself
must have died around 1938,
just before Pa's visit to India in
1939. She had two children—
Dawood and Sulaiman. None

Mum with the Jeewa women in front of their house, Umarwada, 1998.

of them had been to South Africa. Because of the dates of
Fatima and her husband's death, she must have been older than
Pa and possibly of the same father as Pa and his brother, Jeewa
Ishaq Moolla.

AISHABAI AHMED BEMAT

Pa's other sister, Aishabai, was born of his mother, Amaboo's,
second marriage to Mohamed Ebrahim Kazee. She was born in
Umarwada and married Ahmed Ebrahim Bemat. The couple came
to South Africa and settled in Stanger, Natal. The choice to settle
in Stanger does not appear to be random. It was where Pa started
in business in 1899 with his brother
and where his brother had settled and
died. As mentioned above, it is also
where his descendents still live.

Aishabai and her husband,
Ahmed Ebrahim Bemat, had four
children—Goolam Mohamed Ahmed
(born around 1917), Khadija (born
around 1919), Maryam (born around
1927) and Fatima (born in 1933).[71]
According to Mum, her uncle Ahmed

Aishabai Ahmed Bemat, circa 1956.

[71] MSCE 20377/1933 Bemat, Ahmed Ebrahim. (s/sp Ayesha) 1933. Estate
Papers.

Ebrahim Bemat was killed in a Zulu uprising at Chaka's Kraal (Groutville) Natal, but his death notice states that he died after "an accident" on 13 December 1933, in the Indian Immigration Hospital, Lower Tugela District, Stanger. He had made a will on 6 December, a week before his death and presumably in anticipation of it, signed by two witnesses from Groutville, Mahomed Suleman Kajee and Ebrahim Mahomed Kajee, and an Ebrahim Moosa Patel from Stanger. Whether the witnesses were relations is not stated.

According to Pa's immigration file, he applied for a permit to visit Natal in 1933, for the first time since his arrival in South Africa in 1902. He applied for a permit for himself and his son, Ahmed, in February 1934, presumably to be with his sister after the tragic death of her husband two months earlier. Ahmed also died in 1933, and it is not clear whether this was after the proposed visit or whether his death actually put paid to the visit. Mum remembers that Ma also went to Natal to visit Pa's relations, but not being Indian and being born in South Africa, she would not have needed a permit to travel, so it's not possible to know if this was the occasion of that visit.

Pa's sister, Aishabai, returned to India to her home village of Umarwada with her three daughters after the death of her husband, possibly in 1934. She never remarried. After Pa died in 1957, I came across a letter in Gujarati that she had written to him, from which I got her address in Umarwada. I wrote to her, anxious that the link with Pa's family should not be broken, as she was then his only surviving sister. She replied and a correspondence started between us that continued until her death in the late 1960s. We exchanged photos and she sent me the addresses of her daughters, the older two—Khatija and Maryam— by then being married and with children closer to my own age to correspond with.

THE GANGATS

Auntie Khadija, the eldest daughter, married Dawood Mohamed Gangat, a civil servant in the Bombay Government, and the couple settled in Dongri, a suburb of Mumbai. For a short while around 1962, he was the District Excise Inspector for the State of Gujarat and was based at Broach (Bharuch). The couple had four children—Amina (born around 1941), Mohamed Dawood (born in 1943), Khairunissa (born in 1947) and Shabir Ahmed (born around 1954). Auntie Khadija's husband, Dawood Mohamed Gangat, died around 2005/6, and Auntie Khadija moved to Karachi, Pakistan, to stay with her daughter, Amina

THE PATELS

Auntie Maryam, Aishabai's second daughter, married Yusuf Hussain Patel, also from Umarwada, but the couple moved to Karachi after their marriage. They have three sons—Hussain (born around 1947), Farooq (born around 1951) and Mohamed Ashraf (born around 1957).

Maryam Patel, born Bemat, and her husband, Yusuf Hussain Patel, 2010.

Hussain and Muhammad Ashraf both qualified as engineers and at first worked in the Persian Gulf but moved to the United States in the 1970s. Auntie Maryam and Uncle Yusuf Hussain also moved to the States to be near their children, and they now spend the winters in Miami, Florida, with their daughter, Razia, and their summers in Chicago with their son, Mohamed Ashraf.

Standing: Muhammad Ashraf, Hussain and Farooq. Seated: Meher Banu, Auntie Maryam, Uncle Yusuf, and Razia.

The latter is project engineer with Brown Printing Company in Illinois, the fourth largest printing company in the United States.

Standing: Ayesha, Noreen and Muhammad Ameen, with their grandparents, 2010.

They also have two daughters—Meher Banu (born around 1950) and Razia (born around 1955).

Muhammad Ashraf married his first cousin, Nasreen, the daughter of his mother's youngest sister, Fatima. The couple have two children—Ayesha (named after their maternal grandmother, Aishabai) and Mohamed Ameen.

THE BHAYATS

Auntie Fatima, Aishabai's youngest daughter, was born in Stanger, South Africa, in 1933, months before her father died. She grew up in Umarwada and married Mohamad Ismail Bhayat. After their marriage they moved to Karachi, Pakistan. I have a letter written by him dated 13 June 1959 in which he explained the connections of the Bemat family to me, upon which much of this work is based. We lost touch when I became engrossed in my medical studies and then my exile in the 1960s, and it was with great regret that I heard he passed away suddenly on 1 January 2010. The couple have a son and a daughter—Saeed Ahmed and Nasreen. I have mentioned above that Nasreen married her cousin Muhammad Ashraf Patel. I still have the invitation to their wedding on 25 December 1986 at the Babul Islam Masjid, Burns Road, Karachi and the dinner on the following Sunday at the Cosmopolitan Club.

One Sunday afternoon, in the summer of 2008, I received a telephone call from Razia in Miami. Her parents, Auntie Maryam and Uncle Yusuf Hussain Patel, were staying with her at the time. We had a long talk but I was unable to speak to Auntie Maryam as she only spoke Gujarati and I did not know enough Urdu to make a decent conversation. I hope to re-forge the link and perhaps visit them in the States.

THE LE ROUX AND NEL FAMILY

Ma was born Maria Johanna Le Roux on 6 September 1885. Her death notice gives her place of birth as "Cape Province, South Africa", but in Pa's papers, he gave her place of birth on one occasion as Burghersdorp in the Eastern Cape and on another occasion as Hope Town in the Northern Cape, which tallies with oral family history that Ma was born or spent time in Kimberley. Hope Town is not that far from Kimberley, so this story may well turn out to be true.

Ma's parents were Mentor David Le Roux, and Wilhelmina Le Roux. Mentor David was a wagon maker by trade, although the family may have been *Trekboers*(pastoral farmers) in a previous generation. As most travel was done on horseback or by wagon at the time, he would have been much in demand, and this may be the reason why he and his family moved around the Eastern and Northern Cape. David Mentor was born in the District of Graaf Reinet around 1845. His death notice[72] gives his parents as Absalom Le Roux and Anna Le Roux. Little is known about his early life. He married his wife, Wilhelmina Johanna Nel, at Steynsburg in the Eastern Cape. She was a year younger than him and was, therefore, born around 1844. How, when and where they met is not known to me or any of the surviving family.

The 1878 Voters' Roll lists two David Le Roux's. The first one is from the farm Lootsfontein in the Electoral Division of Graaf Reinet. We know that David Mentor was born in the Graaf Reinet district, so this may either be him, his father or his grandfather. In 1878 he would have been about 23 years old and perhaps unlikely to have had enough property to qualify for a vote. My suspicion is that it is probably his grandfather, after whom he may have been named, according to custom. The second David is David Johannes

---

[72] MOOC 6/9/2375 2951 David Mentor Le Roux. Estate Papers. 1922.

Le Roux from the farm Driefontein in the Electoral Division of Colesburg. Graaf Reinet, Steynsburg and Colesburg are not that far apart and further research is needed to tease out the relationships between the three Davids.

David Mentor and Wilhelmina Johanna eventually settled in Grahamstown, and the "Port Elizabeth and Midlands Directory (Grahamstown)" of 1921 has an entry for M(Mentor) D(David) Le Roux, a carter, living at 4 Wylde Street, Grahamstown.[73] This property still exists and as mentioned above was owned by Ma and Pa until 1957. David Mentor died on 4 April 1922 at the age of 77 and is buried in the Old Cemetery, Grahamstown. The index to the records of O D Inggs Undertakers, records that the funeral was conducted by the Independent Church.[74] It is not clear when Wilhelmina Johanna died, but she was only a year younger than him, so it could not have been much later. They are buried side by side in a plot bought for them by Ma, and their graves are surrounded by a small wall which still survives, although there is no headstone.

David Mentor and his wife had a large family of 10 children—Absalom/Aupdoil, Mahomed/Dr Abdol, Maria Johanna (Ma), Anne, Jaftha, Mentor, Willem, Elizabeth, Marthinus, Wilhelmina and Jacobus. According to his death notice, the last three were minors at the time of his death in 1922.

As pointed out above, the family seemed to continue the custom of naming their children after parents or grandparents, hence Absalom was named after his paternal grandfather, Absalom; Anne was named after her paternal grandmother, Anna Le Roux; Mentor was named after his father, David Mentor; and Wilhelmina after her mother, Wilhelmina Johanna. It is tempting to extrapolate from this that Ma must have been named after her maternal grandmother, who would then be Maria Johanna Nel!

---

[73] Port Elizabeth and Midlands Directory (Grahamstown), 1921.
[74] Index To O D Inggs Undertakers, in Cory Library, Rhodes University, Grahamstown.

DR ABDOL AND HIS FAMILY

Absalom/ Aupdoil Mahomed/Dr Abdol was the eldest of the boys. His death notice[75] gives his place of birth as Dassiefontein, probably a farm in the Richmond District of the Eastern Cape. I have pointed out above how his parents moved around the Eastern and Northern Cape. He was a very successful herbalist, hence the "Dr Abdol". I have been unable to find out where or how he obtained his qualifications as a herbalist. He lived next door to his parents at 3 Wylde Street, another property that remained in our family until 1957. He married Magdalena Margarita Dupreez, the daughter of Daniel Dupreez and Annie Klein. According to their marriage certificate, dated 22 February 1926, she was born on 16 March 1896 and had been baptised in the Dutch Reformed Church. She was 12 years younger than him and, interestingly, they were married by a Catholic priest from St Mary's Catholic Church, Grahamstown[76] in their home about a week before he died. He was only 42 and obviously seriously ill when they married.

They must have been living together for a number of years before marrying, because they too had a large family of eight children, only six of whom survived. A reason why they married literally on his deathbed is that her parents may have disapproved of the match and withheld their consent to a marriage. Their eldest daughter, Annie, born on 16 December 1911 and named after her maternal grandmother, Annie Klein, died a day later. The next child, a daughter named Maria, was born on 2 January 1913 and died about three weeks later on 28 January 1913. The third daughter, Wilhelmina, was born on 2 April 1914. She may have been named after her paternal grandmother, Wilhelmina Johanna Le Roux. The next daughter, Annie, born on 27 June 1915, was probably named after her deceased elder sister, Annie. The next child was a boy named Mentor, after his paternal grandfather,

---

[75] MOOC 6/9/2928 10610. Aupdoil Mahomed Le Roux. Estate Papers. 1926.
[76] St Mary's Catholic Church Marriage Registers in the Cory Library, Rhodes University, Grahamstown.

David Mentor Le Roux. He was born on 10 March 1918, about two months before his paternal first cousin, Fatima Ismail, my Mum! After him came another daughter, Maria, born on 1 September 1919 and named after her elder deceased sister, Maria. Their youngest daughter, born on 16 January 1923, was Magdelina, named after her mother, Magdelina Le Roux. The youngest son, Aupdoil Mahomed, was born on 6 October 1924. Dr Abdol obviously followed the tradition of naming children after other members of the family and, hence, the names have survived.

Dr Abdol was wealthy by the standards of the day, and apart from the house next door to his parents in Wylde Street, where he and his family lived and where he died, he also owned a house at 80 Graham Street and one at 49 Wylde Street, all of which my grandparents bought and which remained in the family until 1957. In this era before motor cars, he owned three Scotch carts, one buggy and a four-wheeled cart. Among his livestock were three horses, two mares, four donkeys, four dry cows, eleven cows with calves, and two heifers. Despite his work as a herbalist, he must have retained a love of animal husbandry that is a throwback to the family's origins as pastoralists.

For me a very tangible link with Dr Abdol was one of his daughters. I curse the use of nicknames, as this has now prevented me from knowing exactly which of his daughters she was. We knew her as "Aunt Rice" and she lived opposite the college in Caldecotte Street, Grahamstown, about 200 yards from the Albany Road Cemetery. Often on a Sunday afternoon, after we had visited the family graves, we would walk home, passing her house, and Mum would pop in to see her if she happened to be home. She was of course Mum's first cousin. Aunt Rice was short in stature and on the plump side. She was very fair, blue-eyed and quite charming. She was quite reserved and I never knew her to visit her aunt, Ma. As her sister Annie was known as such, and her other sister Wilhelmina, known as Aunt Min, she was either Maria, born on 1 September 1919 or Magdelina, born on 26 January 1923, both near contemporaries of Mum, who was born in 1918.

ANNIE LE ROUX AND HER FAMILY

Ma's eldest sister was Anne/Annie. She was born on 28 February 1859. She must have been named after her paternal grandmother, Anna Le Roux. She was the same height and build as Ma, and she was as stern and dour as Ma could be. I remember as a child being sent to her house with messages from Ma. She first married Qasim Ismail, a Gujarati businessman, and they had four children—Jainub/Cookie (born on 6 October 1910), Hassan, Ismail and Elizabeth. I remember Jainub quite well, as Aunt Anne, her mother, lived with her and I had to run errands to their house. The couple separated and she married a Hindu, Shanah Naron, by whom she had another daughter, Marion. Aunt Anne died in 1976 at the age of 96! All of Aunt Anne's children and grandchildren were dark in complexion and there is a very marked and strong family resemblance.

The SHA family

Jainub/Cookie, Aunt Anne's eldest daughter, also married a Gujarati businessman, Mohamed Sha. They had six children—Fatima/Fatso, Halima/Liema, Cassim, Sahib, Hoosen, Bokkie and the youngest, Hawa. Oral family history has it that Mohamed Sha wanted to return to Gujarat and take his family with him, but Cookie refused to go. The marriage ended and he eventually settled in Durban, where he married again. Apparently, he kept in touch with the children and often asked them to come and join him and his new family in Durban. Fatima intimated to me on my visit to Grahamstown in April 2010 that she took up the invitation to go to Durban when she was about 21 and stayed with him and his new family but that she found it difficult to adjust and returned

Rush and Cassiem Sha, with the Albany Road Cemetery Grahamstown in the background.

to her mother in Grahamstown after a few months. She too suffers from the familial disease, diabetes, but at the age of more than 80 has a philosophical attitude to the illness and honestly admitted her infringements of her diet.

Liema, the next sister, married a mechanic from Cape Town, Ismail Jattiem. She has diabetes that is difficult to control and she has also recently started to show signs of dementia, which may be diabetes related. The couple continue to live in Grahamstown with their children and grandchildren.

Bokkie, the youngest son, married a pharmacist, Najma Haffejee, and they have three children. Najma came from the same family as Uncle Ebie's ex-wife, Hanifa, and through her, Mum came to know that Hanifa had remarried after her divorce from Uncle Ebie and was now living in Oudtshoorn, on the Garden Route. I don't think Mum ever met her after her divorce from Uncle Ebie, but I do know that Mum never had any rancour towards Hanifa. Sadly, Bokkie also had diabetes and diabetes-related illnesses and died around 2003. Najma and her children continue to live in Grahamstown.

Cassim married Elaine Duiker. He continues to run the general store in Frere Street, opposite Albany Road Cemetery, which his father owned before him. He is in poor health because of his diabetes and the complications of the disease. He and Elaine have four children. I am in touch by email with his married daughter, Faziela, who now lives with her husband and child in Centurion, Pretoria. Sadly, Elaine died of a very malignant cancer on 22 June 2006 and is buried in the Le Roux plot in the Albany Road Cemetery.

Marion Naron

I met Aunt Marion at her home in Grahamstown when Mum, Rush and I visited the graves in 1998. She was a dark-complexioned woman who insisted on living alone, despite her age. I think a compromise was reached when Liema and her husband, Ismail, converted the basement of their house into a granny flat where she could live undisturbed but still within earshot of them in the case of an emergency. She, like many of her family, was greatly in awe of Mum and her family, and considered herself and her family "the poor relations". In fact, she recalled how Auntie used to visit the graves in Grahamstown, staying with her. Auntie would bring the ingredients of a meal but insist that Marion cook the meal for them both while she went off to visit all the Hindu families

Marion Naron (Mum's cousin) and Sonny, Port Alfred, circa 1998.

and "did her own thing"! Marion could not object and would just have to get on with it! Mum often did the same, and she was again powerless to resist! It took a great deal of bullying and threats to persuade her to come with us to Port Alfred for lunch (the infamous "Le Roux stubbornness" we all suffer from!). She visited Mum at 28 Goldsmith Road the following year, literally months before she died. She too is buried in the Le Roux plot in the Albany Road Cemetery. I remember her nephew Bokkie ringing Mum, as "owner" of the plot, for permission to bury her there in one of the family graves. She had never married.

Of Jainub/Cookie's two other sons, Hoosen still lives in Grahamstown. He is divorced and lives on his own. His son lives in Cape Town with his girlfriend and they have two children. I only met them briefly in April 2010, when I attended Fow's graduation in Grahamstown. Fow had got to know Hoosen quite well when she attended Rhodes University, and used to stay with him when she came to Rhodes from East London for her intensive tutorials.

The other son, Sahib, lives in Goodwood, Cape Town, and is apparently very ill with cancer. I have never met him.

DAVID MENTOR LE ROUX'S OTHER CHILDREN

Jaftha Le Roux

There are only two of Ma's other brothers and sisters that I know fairly well. Great-uncle Jaftha (or Boetie Jaftha) had a reputation as a heavy drinker. He worked on farms as a *knecht* (supervisor of the workers), with responsibility for running the farm on behalf of the owners. He would occasionally come into town and stay with various relatives. He was a tall man, very fair, with red hair. The surname Le Roux originally meant "the red one" in French, referring to the colour of the hair and beard, and in this respect Great-uncle Jaftha was a true Le Roux! Uncle Sol looked very much like him. I met him on one of these visits when he turned up at Ma and Pa's shop in Beaufort Street the worse for wear. He was very unceremoniously put to bed in the basement of the house next to the shop (number 10 Beaufort Street) to sober up and told in no uncertain terms by Ma the next day that he was not welcome to visit in that state, especially with her grandchildren around! I never saw him again but heard from Auntie in the 1960s that he had died. I don't think he ever married.

Elizabeth Wessels, formerly Hendricks, born Le Roux

Ma's sister, Elizabeth, or Aunt Beth as we knew her, was quite a different kettle of fish. She was the same in build and stature as Ma and Aunt Anne and similar in complexion. Whereas the latter were strong, rather dour, women, Aunt Beth was very much softer in temperament, more easily approachable and appeared to be more fun loving. I first met her in the early 1950s when Ma visited us at 59 Fenton Road, Salt River. The two of them had travelled together by train from Grahamstown and I think Ma had wanted company for the long train journey; at the time, it took three days and two nights by train! The previous time Ma had visited, Uncle Ebie had accompanied her.

Aunt Beth was an immediate hit with Bie and his family. She hit it off particularly well with Bie, and they had many a laugh together. Whereas with Ma Bie had always been respectful and slightly shy and deferential, he could be more relaxed with Aunt Beth. She was good with us children as well. She took over looking after us, washing and dressing us and feeding us, and of course protecting us from the displeasure of our parents when we were naughty. She visited us again the following year, this time on her own, and everyone had a ball!

She had what we fondly call the "Le Roux gene of obsessive cleanliness" and did not flinch from dismissing Mum's domestic helper and doing all the housework and laundry herself! She had been married to a Mr Hendricks, who I never knew and who was never spoken of. She married again, a widower, Cotties Wessels from Fort Beaufort, with whom she found great happiness. His children were quite small when they married but she accepted them as her own and brought them up with all the love and kindness of a birth mother. She and her husband were quite active in the United Congregational Church, but a rift occurred and they left the Church.

I was warmly received by Aunt Beth's daughter-in-law, despite her poor health, on a visit to Fort Beaufort in 2007. She kindly allowed me to have a copy of a photo of Aunt Beth and Uncle Cotties on their wedding day. It shows Aunt Beth as a slim and very beautiful woman, confident at her new husband's side. Aunt Beth's daughter-in-law was a wealth of information about their life in Fort Beaufort. Apparently, Uncle Cotties had been a builder, but work had dried up after the war and he had had to find another means of supporting his family. He and Aunt Beth then opened a laundry together and had the monopoly of the business in Fort Beaufort for some years. She would do all the washing and ironing using the traditional methods of boiling and bleaching. He was the first person to own a car in Fort Beaufort and did the deliveries in it! They both died in the 1970s. A rather tragic thing occurred a few years before her death. Her younger brother, Marthinus Le Roux, who lived in Middledrift in the Eastern Cape at the time, came to visit her and died rather unexpectedly. She is now buried next to him in the cemetery at Fort Beaufort. According to her

Elizabeth Wessels (Aunt Beth), born Le Roux, and her husband, Cotties Wessels.

daughter-in-law, his family are still in Middledrift. She described them as "very dour" and "old-style Afrikaners", and according to her, they too had the Le Roux red hair!

I have not met any of Ma's other brothers and sisters or their descendents yet, although there must be many scattered around the Eastern Cape. Oral history has it that one of her brothers fought in the Korean War, but I've been unable to verify this yet and the search continues.

Jacobus Le Roux

Jacobus, or Cobus, was the youngest of Ma's brothers, born around 1899. He is said to have been a minor when his father, Mentor David, died in 1922. In fact, he was about 13 years old. He married when he was 21, and I came across his marriage certificate[77] quite by chance. He was married in St Mary's Catholic Church by special dispensation, obtained on 13 August 1920, as he belonged to the Union Church, while his fiancée was presumably a Catholic. She was a Sara Thomas, the daughter of Alfred Thomas and Anna Wessels. She was 17 when the marriage took place. Jacobus died at his home, 1 Cobden Street, Grahamstown, on 11 January 1928 and is buried in the Albany Street Cemetery, the burial being conducted by the Union Church.[78] The Catholic priest at St Mary's who married them added a note in pencil to the certificate, saying that Sara had "run off with a Malay", but exactly when is not clear. Jacobus was only 28 when he died, and it is unclear whether he and Sara had any children.

Wilhelmina Le Roux

Wilhelmina was probably the youngest of all of Mentor David's children and may have been around five years old when he died.

---

[77] Marriage Registers of St Mary's Catholic Church, Grahamstown. The Cory Library, Rhodes University.
[78] Index to the records of O D Inggs Undertakers, Grahamstown. The Cory Library, Rhodes University.

Sadly, I have only been able to find the record of her death and burial. She died on 13 October 1927 and is buried with the rest of the family in the Albany Street Cemetery.[79]

THE LE ROUX ORIGINS

The Le Roux are one of the largest Afrikaner families of Huguenot descent in South Africa. There are two branches of the family. The first branch originated in Blois, France, from where two brothers migrated to the Cape via Holland. Jean Le Roux, born in 1667 in Blois, arrived at the Cape on the *Voorschoten* on 13 April 1688, making him one of the first of the French Huguenots to arrive at the Cape. He married Jeanne Mouy and they had four children. He died in 1711, and from him and his wife is descended one branch of the family.

His younger brother, Gabriel Le Roux, was born in 1671 and also arrived in South Africa in 1688. He married Maria Catharina Le Febre, by whom he had two children, and from them is descended another branch of the family. He too died in 1711.

A third branch of the family is descended from Jean Le Roux of Normandy. He is a contemporary of the other two Le Roux brothers.

THE NELS

Ma's mother, Wilhelmina Johanna Le Roux, born Nel, was born around 1844. Her parents were Hendrik and Maria Nel. We have a black and white photo of the couple showing them as a rather stern-looking pair staring out at the camera. He has a long white beard, while she is dressed in a simple dark dress with a lace collar. She has her hair tied tightly back. They look like any Afrikaner couple of their time. I do not know if Mum ever met her great-grandparents, but she always spoke of them in hushed tones. I once overheard a story that when Ma's mother, Wilhelmina

---

[79] Index to the records of O D Inggs Undertakers, Grahamstown. Cory Library, Rhodes University.

Hendrik and Maria Nel.

Johanna, visited her parents she would have to address them as "Mr and Mrs Nel". It seems they disapproved of her marriage to David Mentor Le Roux. I don't think the feud was ever resolved.

I suspect that they too were pastoralists, but they may well have owned a farm. They certainly lived in the frontier country of the Eastern Cape, probably at Steynsburg, where their daughter, Ma's mother, and David Mentor Le Roux married. Branches of the Le Roux and Nel families were part of the *voortrekkers* (discontented colonists) who decided to move North and East of the Cape Colony and into the interior, away from British colonial rule. It may well be that Hendrik and Maria came from one of these families. In the absence of their second given names, it becomes harder to place them more accurately, but if they followed the custom, Maria's second name may have been Johanna and Ma would have been named after her maternal grandmother, Maria Johanna Nel.

The Nel family too are descendents of the French Huguenots of 1688 and are as numerous in South Africa today as the Le Roux. There are again two branches of the family, one descended from Guillaume Nel and the other from Etienne Nel. The latter was born in the Dauphinè, France, in 1668 and married Marie Madelaine Marais from Hierpoix in 1682. Some assert that Guillaume and Etienne were brothers, so the two branches of the Nel family are genetically linked, whereas this is not necessarily so in the case of the Le Roux. More information and research is needed to clarify the Nel connections.

THE FAMILY IN THE YEAR 2010

I have set down as much of the origin of the family as I have been able to research to date and have pointed out the many areas that need further investigation. It has helped and pleasantly surprised me that many oral sources have proved to have had more than an element of verifiable truth in them, and they have frequently pointed the direction to the search of the historical records. As the elder generation die out, this source of information will become more tenuous, unreliable and just not available, so I make an appeal to everyone in the family to add to the story by recording as much as is possible for the next generation of researchers.

Of course, there are many gaps in the historical records, but since 1994, when all archival records in South Africa became available to the general public, a great deal of verifiable information is now in the public domain and available to interested researchers, and more and more will become so each year, especially in what one previously thought of as "unproductive" fields like "slave history". The loss of identity and de-personalisation of slaves made it very difficult, if not impossible, in the past to follow up leads, but I am optimistic that as more archival material comes to light, this problem can be overcome.

I am concerned that whatever is already available in the archives should be preserved in the best possible way for the next generations and continue to be as freely available as they are now. It is regrettable that there are so many files with documents "missing" or "defaced", and the loss of valuable information is distressing, impeding as it does the search for knowledge and clarity.

It is difficult to tease out the role of "nature or nurture" in the disease patterns of any individual or group of individuals. We know that certain conditions, like high levels of cholesterol in the blood, do run in families and may predispose to particular illnesses, like heart attacks and stroke. The Salasas and the Ismails are no strangers to these diseases and I am sure that both genetics and environment contributed to the incidence of these diseases in both families for many decades. It is on record that Adonis of the Cape, and possibly Willem of the Cape too, in the first part of the 19th century, were in their sixties when they died. Sarina Salassa and her daughter Gadija were also in their sixties when they died, and as I pointed out, all of Gadija's sons surviving into adulthood, except one, died before they were 60. We do not know how old Abas Salassa was when he died, but his son Rajab was also only

60 when he died. This does not negate the fact that a healthy diet and exercise, among other things, can be helpful in keeping these "familial illnesses" at bay, but the genetic element here is a strong one.

It is a truism that there is no such thing as a "pure race". We are all the products of intermarriage, as people migrated and spread over the continents for thousands of years. The claim of descent from "a pure racial line" is, therefore, utter nonsense. For too long in South Africa have we been indoctrinated to think of ourselves and our self-worth in terms of our racial descent and the colour of our skin, and it may take as many generations as it took for us to be so indoctrinated to rid ourselves of that prejudice. The Salasa family too, like many other families in South Africa, are clearly descended from many immigrant sources, whether slaves from the Dutch colonies in Batavia, India, Ceylon, Mauritius and the Far East, or European settlers from Holland or France. All of these sources have made us what we are today and enriched our lives by their different religions, languages and cultures. It should dispel from our minds any ideas of cultural, religious or racial superiority and should make us proud of our diversity and cultural heritage. Above all, one should beware of scorning or looking down on anyone; they may be your cousin twice removed!

REFERENCES

DOCUMENTARY SOURCES.

The Cape Town Archive Repository

CO   Colonial Office

CSC   Cape Supreme Court

DOC   Registrar of Deeds

IRC   Immigration Restriction Department

J   Opgaafrollen/Census Records VOC

MOIB   Records of Insolvent Estates

MOIC   Records of Insolvent Liquidation and Distribution
        Accounts

MOOC   Records of Deceased Estates

NCD   Notarial Records of Individual Notaries

SO   Slave Office

Pietermaritzburg Archive Repository

IND
MSCE   Master of the Supreme Court Deceased Estates

Selected Bibliography

Bank, A., *The Decline of Urban Slavery at the Cape, 1806-1843*, Cape Town, Centre for African Studies, University of Cape Town, 1991.

Bickford-Smith, V., *Ethnic Pride and Racial Prejudice in Victorian Cape Town*, Cambridge, Cambridge University Press, 1995.

Böeseken, *Anna J. Slaves and Free Blacks at the Cape, 1658–1700*, Cape Town, Tafelberg, 1977.

Bradlow, Frank R., and Margaret Cairns, *The Early Cape Muslims: A Study of Their Mosques, Genealogy and Origins*, Cape Town, Balkema, 1978.

Davids, Achmat, *The History of the Tana Baru*, Cape Town, The Committee for the Preservation of the Tana Baru, 1985.

Davids, Achmat, *The Mosques of the Bo-Kaap*, Athlone, The South African Institute of Arabic and Islamic Research, 1980.

Dooling, W., *Slavery, Emancipation and Colonial Rule in South Africa*, University of Kwazulu-Natal Press, 2007.

Elphick, R. and Giliomee, H. (eds.), *The Shaping of South African Society 1652–1840 (2nd edition)*, Cape Town, Maskew Miller Longman, 1989.

Heese, Hans Friedreich, *Groep Sonder Grense: Die rol en status van die gemengde bevolking aan die Kaap, 1652–1795*. Bellville, Wes Kaaplandse Instituut vir Historiese Navorsing, 1984.

Leibbrandt, Hendrik Carel Vos. Requesten (Memorials) 1715–1806. 5 vols. Cape Town, 1905; Cape Town: South African Library, 1989.

Marais, J.S., *The Cape Coloured People 1652–1937*, Johannesburg, Witwatersrand University Press, 1968, first published 1939.

Mason, J. E., *Social Death and Resurrection: Slavery and Emancipation in South Africa*, London, University of Virginia Press, 2003.

Pama, C., comp., and De Villiers, C. C., *Geslagsregisters van die ou Kaapse Families*, 2 vols, Cape Town, Balkema, 1981.

Plessis du, Izaak David, *The Cape Malays: History, Religion, Traditions, Folk Tales, the Malay Quarter* (3rd edition), Cape Town, Balkema, 1972.

Ross, R., *Cape of Torments: Slavery and Resistance in South Africa*, London, Routledge, 1983.

Shell, R. C-H, *Children of Bondage: A Social History of the Slave Society at the Cape of Good Hope, 1652–1838*, Johannesburg, Witwatersrand University Press, 1994.

Worden, N., *Slavery in Dutch South Africa*, Cambridge, Cambridge University Press, 1985.

Worden, N and Crais C., (eds.), *Breaking the Chains: Slavery and its Legacy in the Nineteenth-century Cape Colony*, Johannesburg, Witwatersrand University Press, 1994.

Worden, N., van Heyningen, E., and Bickford-Smith, V., *Cape Town, The Making of a City: An Illustrated History*, Cape Town, David Philip, 1998.

Newspapers

The Cape Argus

The Cape Times

Grocott's Daily Mail (Grahamstown)

The Author

Mohamed Hassan Salasa, also known as Sonny Salasa, was born in Cape Town and completed his primary and secondary education at Habibia Kokhani Educational Institute and Trafalgar High School respectively before graduating MB ChB from the University of Cape Town's Medical School in December 1967. He completed his pre-registration house jobs in Medicine and Surgery at the Lusaka Central, now the University Teaching Hospital, Lusaka, in 1968. He returned to the United Kingdom to train in Psychiatry, and has lived there ever since.

He obtained the Diploma in Psychiatric Medicine (DPM) in July 1972 and Membership of the Royal College of Psychiatrists (MRCPsych) in November 1972. After training in psychiatry at the Royal Free, Guy's, and the Bethlem and Maudsley Hospitals in London, he became Consultant Psychiatrist at Hill End and St Albans City Hospitals, St Albans, Hertfordshire, in 1978. He worked briefly at St Crispin's Hospital, Northampton, and Stevenage Hospital, North Hertfordshire, before his retirement in December 1997.

In 1999 he enrolled at the School of Oriental and African Studies (SOAS) of the University of London and graduated BA (Hons) in Persian and Arabic in 2005.

Lightning Source UK Ltd.
Milton Keynes UK
UKHW021139181222
414024UK00011B/256

9 781803 812717